AIRBORNE

the
DAMON STOUDAMIRE
STORY

DOUG SMITH

VIKING

VIKING
Published by the Penguin Group
Penguin Books Canada Ltd, 10 Alcorn Avenue, Toronto, Ontario, Canada M4V 3B2
Penguin Books Ltd, 27 Wrights Lane, London W8 5TZ, England
Viking Penguin, a division of Penguin Books USA Inc., 375 Hudson Street, New
York, New York 10014, U.S.A.
Penguin Books Australia Ltd, Ringwood, Victoria, Australia
Penguin Books (NZ) Ltd, cnr Rosedale and Airborne Roads, Albany, Auckland
1310, New Zealand

Penguin Books Ltd, Registered Offices: Harmondsworth, Middlesex, England

First published 1997

1 3 5 7 9 10 8 6 4 2
Copyright © Doug Smith and Damon Stoudamire, 1997

Printed and bound in Canada on acid free paper

Canadian Cataloguing in Publication Data

Smith, Doug, 1958–
    Airborne: the Damon Stoudamire story

ISBN 0-670-87640-2

1. Stoudamire, Damon. 2. Toronto Raptors (Basketball team). 3. Basketball
players—Ontario—Toronto—Biography. I. Title.

GV884.S76864 1997   796.323'092   C97-930557-8

Designed and typeset by Rocket Design

Visit Penguin Canada's web site at www.penguin.ca

ACKNOWLEDGMENTS

My deepest thanks to Damon for his honesty and openness during the creation of this book.

And to Susan Walsh, my wife and best friend, for her unwavering support and incredible patience through every step of the journey.

Finally, to Jacob, our son, and pride and joy, who can now see what his daddy has been doing all these months.

CONTENTS

INTRODUCTION

ISIAH ON DAMON

BY ISIAH THOMAS

WHEN I BECAME PART-OWNER and Executive Vice President, Basketball, of the Toronto Raptors Basketball Club, I became intent on finding the formula that would allow me to build a team capable of winning an NBA championship. As a player with the Detroit Pistons, I was able to realize that dream twice. However, I was now stepping into a totally different domain — the world of management. Fortunately, I have received a great deal of sound advice throughout my life. So I pulled out all the knowledge that had been passed on to me over the years and looked for that one piece of guidance that would help me begin this building process.

I was once told that when you are putting something together, each and every piece is important. However, there are two pieces that stand above the rest — the cornerstone, the first piece of the foundation, and the keystone, the final piece that holds all the others in place. These parts are the beginning and the end, the necessary components that complete the team. Knowing this was one thing; going out and finding those pieces would be the real challenge.

I first watched Damon Stoudamire play while he was at the University of Arizona during the NCAA Final Four in 1994. I was impressed by his incredible speed, exceptional ball-handling and stamina. His court sense quickly caught my attention. What I was seeing was the consummate floor general. He seemed to have a strategy in place. He knew his teammates well, distributed the ball, and used his creativity and quickness to advantage over larger opponents.

Since we were an expansion team, I was starting from scratch. I would be drafting both current NBA players through the expansion draft and college players through the annual NBA draft. I kept a close eye on Damon during his senior year at Arizona, and although I attended numerous college games that season and pored over tapes of players, Damon was always in the back of my mind. He had the skills that separated him from the rest of the pack. I felt very strongly that if he was around when my pick came up, I would draft him.

In June 1995 we brought Damon to Toronto for a workout before the draft. We were astounded — he blew away the standards for our physical tests. For example, we usually ask for thirty or forty push-ups. Damon easily reached this number; he was heading towards eighty when he looked up at me to ask if he should keep going.

For me, though, there was something beyond Damon's physical abilities. I watched the way he carried himself and the way he approached the game. He had a quality that I couldn't quite put my finger on, but I knew it was something special.

Later that same month, it was time for the college draft. Luckily, the six teams ahead of us focused on selecting size, and we were able to secure Damon with the seventh pick. My first piece was in place; I had drafted the cornerstone.

Many critics argued with my selection of Damon because of his small stature, but I couldn't wait for people to see him play. In our opening game in Halifax, Nova Scotia, in October 1995, Damon exploded for 20 points in the first half against the Philadelphia 76ers, and he hasn't looked back since. The respect he earned in his first season won him the NBA Rookie of the Year award.

Damon's immense mental and emotional depth has struck

me only over time. During our second season, we suffered a 113–86 loss to the Washington Bullets in late March. With only a month left in the season and some tough games on the road ahead, most teams would have just let the season run out. It looked as if our team would do the same. But Damon was on board, and he would not let the ship go down.

The following day, Damon called a players-only team meeting behind closed doors. For a second-year player, that was very unusual; these meetings are usually called by veterans. He urged his teammates to communicate and commit themselves for the remainder of the season, regardless of the fact that we were out of the playoff race. The team came out the next day to beat the Miami Heat, a team that was on an eight-game winning streak and would eventually go to the Eastern conference finals. I now understand what I was sensing during that first workout. You see, everyone hates to lose, but Damon hates to lose more than most people. He is a fiercely competitive person.

Sure, Damon Stoudamire is unique because he's five-foot-ten and playing in a league where the average height of a player is six-foot-eight. Yet there is so much more to him than that. Damon is about hard work, intensity, toughness and determination. He's the kind of athlete who would still be playing this game even if he wasn't collecting a paycheque. His strong convictions and unassuming leadership define what our organization is all about. He is our rare natural resource, and he will go to any lengths to win. He will not stop until he's reached that ultimate goal, an NBA championship.

As we enter our third season, I realize there will still be some pieces to add to my structure. However, I've found that other important piece. Damon Stoudamire, with his maturity and his leadership, has now also emerged as our keystone — the final piece that supports and holds all the others in place.

Now that is what being rare is all about.

DRAFT NIGHT

I T'S A HOT WEDNESDAY NIGHT in late June, and the SkyDome is decked out as never before. The home team's brand new basketball court, with its nifty little dinosaur tracks running diagonally from one corner to the other, is about to host the NBA's 1995 college draft.

At one time, the annual allotting of college players to the league's franchises was held in a boardroom at the league's New York offices. But these days, the draft is big business, big entertainment. The NBA decided in 1992 to take its show on the road — first to Portland, then Detroit, then Indiana and finally to Toronto.

A huge stage dominates the middle of the expansive

SkyDome floor, flanked by mini-television studios ready to beam the night's festivities around the world. Various team officials and league functionaries are scurrying to and fro, testing the sound systems, checking out the scoreboard, running through the script to be followed by players and officials. Neither the fans at home nor the people in the stadium will abide any screw-ups. This is a co-production between the league and a franchise that has never staged an event before, and it has to go off without a hitch.

As the doors open to the public, tens of thousands of fans flock to their seats. Most are teenagers, who represent the basketball subculture of a hockey-mad city. Some are adults whose curiosity has been tweaked by the marketing wizardry of the most successful sports league in the world. Some people have come just to see what all the fuss is about.

Until this evening, the Toronto Raptors have been little more than a name, a logo, a colour scheme and a lot of question marks. Born in the boardroom in 1994, the team has yet to play a game. But that doesn't matter to the people who are already fans of the fledgling franchise. Tickets for the coming season have been sold and promises have been made primarily on the outcome of this night. *Trust us*, is the team's unspoken credo, *we'll do the right thing. We'll get the right players.*

So far, the team's roster contains nothing more than the

rejects of other teams — the Acie Earls, John Salleys, Tony Massenburgs, Ed Pinckneys and B.J. Tylers of the league. They were plucked from the discard heap a couple of weeks earlier in the expansion draft, an exercise that occurs each time the league adds teams — in this case, the Raptors and the Vancouver Grizzlies. The expansion draft allows established teams to shed unwanted players — some of whom have doubtful skills, others of whom have questionable attitudes, and most of whom have large, guaranteed contracts. Only three players from each of the existing twenty-seven teams were made available, most of them bit players and forgotten names.

Tonight, behind a huge blue backdrop sit the young men who are the evening's main attractions. In freshly pressed suits, with jewellery glistening, they and their families sit at well-appointed tables, making trips every now and then to the abundant buffet laid out for them. They wait for the festivities to begin, for NBA commissioner David Stern to stride across the stage and call their names. They imagine themselves shaking hands and posing for the obligatory picture for the papers back home.

This is a night for the future. This night is for the superstar, the man who will be the first college draft pick in Raptors history, the man with whom the infant team will be forever linked. The 1995 NBA college draft is a time for a star to be born.

And on the floor of the stadium, hidden from the public's view, five-foot, ten-inch Damon Stoudamire smiles a knowing smile.

Up until 1985, drafting order was determined strictly by each team's standing at the end of the previous season. Now, the NBA uses a lottery system that is not pre-set but weighted towards the teams with the worst regular-season records. To ensure the teams continue to give their best effort as the season winds down, the league gives all the non-playoff teams an opportunity to get the first overall choice, and therefore the best player. The team with the worst record has the most chances, the second-worst team the second-most chances, and so on. Thanks to this system, the New York Knicks won the first pick in 1985 and took Patrick Ewing. There is enough movement of teams up and down the order of selection over the years to make this nationally televised event, held about a month before the college draft, a highlight of the off-season.

Before their first season in the league, the Orlando Magic won the 1992 lottery and were able to take the giant Shaquille O'Neal with the number-one selection. A year later, the Magic won the lottery a second time and were able to parlay that victory into the addition of Penny Hardaway to the team, giving it immediate contender status. The other members of the NBA, who watched the upstart Magic reach the NBA finals just six seasons into their existence, vowed not to let that happen again and penalized the Raptors and Grizzlies. Neither team will be eligible for the number-one selection until 1999, according to the expansion agreements they reached with the league. Toronto and Vancouver will select sixth and seventh tonight. Because Vancouver won a coin flip and chose to take the second pick in the expansion draft, the Grizzlies will get the sixth selection of the college stars tonight, Toronto the seventh.

The 1995 draft is focused primarily on kids — four college sophomores and a high school student who are thought to be far and away the best available players of the fifty-eight to be chosen. These five are the centre of attention, and all that's left to be determined is in which order they will be selected.

Joe Smith of the University of Maryland, a month shy of his twentieth birthday, is the most coveted. A gifted forward, the six-foot, eleven-inch prodigy is the consensus number-one pick. The Golden State Warriors, with the fifth-worst record the previous season, have won the NBA's draft lottery, and as the draft begins they surprise no one by taking Smith.

Antonio McDyess of Alabama, coming off a brilliant NCAA

tournament where he impressed scouts with the sheer power contained in his six-foot-nine frame, is another of the highly prized youngsters. The twenty-one-year-old is drafted next, by the sad-sack Los Angeles Clippers. The Clippers, in keeping with their tradition of making decisions that would keep them perennially among the league's worst teams, trade him moments later to the Denver Nuggets, who can hardly believe their luck.

Jerry Stackhouse and Rasheed Wallace, twenty-one-year-old sophomore teammates from the University of North Carolina, are the odds-on favourites to go third and fourth. Stackhouse, a lithe, six-foot-six twenty-one-year-old, is the best pure scorer among the top five choices, a solid outside shooter with the ability to slash to the basket at every opportunity. The Philadelphia 76ers snap him up gleefully.

Wallace, who added power to Stackhouse's grace at North Carolina, is the most talkative and the most animated of this draft's young talent. He is six feet, ten inches and 225 pounds of raw ability, and he knows it. A native of Philadelphia, he would have been a good fit with the Sixers, had they not already had Shawn Bradley in the middle. The Washington Bullets, however, need a centre — someone to bang under the boards — and they use the fourth pick to take Wallace.

Kevin Garnett, who just a month ago was a high school student in Chicago, is the youngest of the young, nineteen

years old and about to make the giant leap from school to the
NBA. Questions abound about his ability to make the social
adjustment from algebra class to the fast-paced life of an NBA
player. Still, his skills are unique — a combination of speed,
power and grace packaged in a still-growing six-foot, eleven-
inch body.

The Minnesota Timberwolves take what is perceived to be a
big risk with the fifth pick. Garnett is a long-term project, but
Kevin McHale, the legendary Boston Celtic forward now
employed as the T-Wolves general manager, is a gambler and
Garnett is on his way to staid, white-bread Minneapolis — a
world away from his Chicago childhood — where he will
eventually lead the Timberwolves to their first playoff appearance in franchise history.

Once those five are gone, the drama and the tension on the
SkyDome floor become palpable. In the SkyDome stands, the
fans are anxious. Nerves are starting to fray. The Grizzlies and
Raptors have the next two picks, and history is about to be
made.

At one table, looking a little lost amid the tuxedos, gold
chains and glitz and glamour is Bryant "Big Country" Reeves,
the small-town, seven-foot Oklahoman whose quiet demeanour
and "aw-shucks" personality belie a competitive nature that sets
him apart from many of the other draft-eligible players. Reeves
is the "safe" pick, a known entity who has spent four full

seasons in college basketball — unusual in these days when juniors, sophomores and even freshmen and high-schoolers are entering the draft. Reeves personifies the basketball saying that you can't teach height, and any questions about his fundamental skills are overshadowed by his sheer physical presence. Grizzlies general manager Stu Jackson, his conservative personality rising to the fore, wants Reeves, and he wastes no time in making the first selection in his franchise's history.

This leaves the smallest of the possible first-round picks, the somewhat forgotten five-foot, ten-inch point guard from the University of Arizona, another senior, who has somehow managed to sneak by many of the pundits. Surrounded by his family — his father, Willie, his mother, Liz Washington, his maternal grandmother, Elizabeth Washington, and his cousin Antoine — and supported by long-time friend Erin Cowan and his girlfriend, Rene Evans, Damon Stoudamire sits calmly. He is on the last leg of an improbable journey from the streets of Portland, Oregon, to the bright lights of the NBA.

After fighting long odds at nearly every turn just to get to Toronto and this night, he is ready. Finally, the moment arrives.

Commissioner David Stern speaks the words the team's fans have waited for since the franchise was awarded in 1994:

"With the seventh pick, their first ever pick, the Toronto Raptors choose Damon Stoudamire from the University of

Arizona."

Boos ring down from the SkyDome stands, boos from uneducated fans who wanted the Raptors to choose a more familiar player — someone like Ed O'Bannon, who led the UCLA Bruins to the NCAA championship two and a half months earlier; someone like Cherokee Parks, another centre who just finished a fine career at Duke, one of the few schools Canadian fans know well. Stoudamire is virtually unheard of by anyone outside the Canadian basketball cognoscenti, a "Who's he?" among the "Who's Who."

Ever since he first picked up a basketball on the playgrounds of Portland, Stoudamire has been silencing critics and sceptics and having a ball doing it. There have been more auspicious debuts than being jeered by your new hometown fans the first time they hear your name, and the boos sting for a moment, but Stoudamire is undaunted.

"I was really happy, but I think he might have been a little leery," says Damon's mother, who is surprised by the reaction — so surprised it takes a couple of seconds to sink in that people are booing her child. "But now I look at it like those boos were a challenge for Damon, again. Every time someone said he couldn't do this, or he was too small, or he couldn't do that, he just went out and proved them wrong. I thought the fans were wrong, and I knew he'd prove it."

When you are a little guy in a big man's game, silencing the critics is almost as much fun as leading a fast break.

"When it happened, I thought, 'Shoot, there are people out there booing. What are they doing?'" recalls Stoudamire. "That was the funniest thing to me. I was laughing at them. I was thinking, 'They must not be basketball knowledgeable in Toronto.' I said I'd show them how wrong they were."

As he had done so many, many times before.

In a crowded room a couple of storeys above the SkyDome floor and hidden from the twenty thousand fans and their opinions, there is a decidedly different reaction. The brain trust of the franchise — general manager, vice-president and part-owner Isiah Thomas, his coaching and scouting staffs and a handful of others — are smiling. They have their man, the opinions of the crowd be damned. They know they are right.

In Stoudamire, lightning quick and possessed of a driven personality that will not accept defeat, they have the man to lead the franchise, the cornerstone of the long, arduous process of building towards a championship.

"We never seriously considered anyone else," says Thomas. "We didn't even want to bring him to work out, we didn't want to tip our hand. There might have been one guy in that room who wanted us to take O'Bannon, and he turned out to be pretty wrong. We were pretty happy when me made that choice."

To them, it was a no-brainer.

"When they say your name, you feel relieved," says Stoudamire, "and you thank God you only have to go through that once.

"I was happy, I got home, I got me a big bottle of wine and I drank my wine for like three days. I had so much fun, and then it was right back to work."

In large part, it's that kind of work ethic that made Stoudamire so attractive to Thomas. Because Thomas was one of the best point guards ever to play the game — two NBA titles with the Detroit Pistons, a litany of franchise records, a reputation as one of the hardest-battling players ever to lace on sneakers — the choice made a lot of sense. If Isiah Thomas is going to build a championship team in Toronto, he wants to build it around a player like himself. Damon Stoudamire is the closest thing to an Isiah Thomas clone to arrive in years.

"All my people were saying stuff like, 'They had to pick you. Do you think Isiah Thomas is going to pick a centre like Big Country or Ed O'Bannon or somebody like that? Hell, no. He's going to pick you because when he sees you play, he sees himself. He sees a young Isiah in you.' I guess it was the logical choice."

It didn't hurt, either, that Stoudamire had absolutely lit up the gym when he held his personal pre-draft workout for the Raptors a month earlier in Toronto.

"When he came in for his private workout, he was by far the strongest guy we had," recalls Thomas. "We had him do pushups, and he kept doing them. We had him do situps, and he just kept doing them. Anything we wanted, he did. And more. He could go on and on and on.

"One thing that surprised us was his vertical leap. He had about a forty-three-inch vertical. He could dunk the basketball. He was the most physically fit guy we had come in. We put him through some shooting drills and he made his first twenty-two shots. We were just amazed by the guy."

Stoudamire took it all in stride. The exceptional private workout for the Raptors was just one of many. When he worked out one-on-one with Florida State's Bob Sura, he beat him so badly that Sura dropped to seventeenth in the draft after being rated much higher; Brent Barry, from Oregon State, was another college player Stoudamire scorched in an NBA audition.

The Portland Trail Blazers were so interested in Stoudamire that they swapped their seventeenth pick with Detroit's number eight, hoping Stoudamire would still be available. In fact, after a chance meeting with an NBA insider in Chicago's O'Hare airport the day before the draft, Liz Washington arrived in Toronto fully expecting her son to be chosen by the Portland team. Danny Ainge, then a television commentator and now the head coach of the Phoenix Suns, told her that the rumour mill was working overtime concerning her son. She had recognized Ainge and asked him about her son's draft prospects.

"He told me he had talked to someone in Portland and that they were going to pick Damon," is how she remembers the conversation. "Personally, I didn't want Damon to play in Portland. Being a rookie in his home town with everybody expecting the world of him, I thought that wouldn't be the best situation for him. But for a while, I was certain that was going to happen."

Damon wasn't.

"I actually wanted to go to Washington at the fourth pick," said Stoudamire. That would have been a perfect fit for a point guard like Stoudamire, because the Bullets had plenty of young talent but lacked a floor leader. But he harbours no disappointment.

"I knew they weren't going to take me because I knew there was too much pressure on them. Everyone was talking about the four sophomores — Wallace, Smith, McDyess and Stack — so I knew they had to take one of those. It worked out okay."

The NBA draft involves much more than just finding the guy you want, waiting for the day to arrive and then picking him. For Thomas, the process began the day he was hired by the NBA's first Canadian franchise. Of course, he began watching for basketball abilities: the way a player made those around him better, the way a young man could put a team on his back and carry it to success.

"When we sat down and talked to Damon, the thing I really liked about him was that right away you could see the passion for basketball, the burning fire for basketball," recalls Thomas.

"The words that kept coming back were workaholic, gym rat, a guy who would stay in the gym forever. A competitive guy, a great team guy, a guy you could count on. It was basketball, basketball, basketball. And that's the kind of stuff that separates the greats from the averages. At twelve o'clock at night, if you called him and said 'Let's go down to the rec centre and play some ball,' he'd go. He isn't playing basketball for the money, he plays the game because he has a sheer love for it. That's what hit us. Damon had it written all over him that he just loved to play. I knew he'd come into the league and not only be good but have a chance to be great."

But there was more. Thomas knew that entrusting the team to a young man fresh out of college was fraught with peril. Many young men can't handle the responsibility, can't handle the fame and can't handle the money. The streets are full of could-have-beens, players who fall by the wayside in a pool of unrealized potential.

"As the first pick of our franchise, and as my first pick as a general manager, he had to check out in every way," says Thomas. "We had to see what his character was like, how he would handle the peripheral stuff that goes with being in the NBA, that goes with being a first-round pick. We talked to his friends, we talked to his coaches, we talked to his opponents — we had to be sure we were getting a quality guy on and off the court, and I think people realize now that we did."

Stoudamire knew there were no demons in his past. He knew — or, at least, hoped — people would admire him for his combativeness, for his hard-working personality, for his dedication to realizing his dream. "It didn't bother me at all," he says. "Everybody's got to get checked up on. I was pretty comfortable about that."

Liz Washington didn't mind the close scrutiny either. She had instilled a sense of responsibility in her only child that set him apart from many other children. She had given him a grounding that made clear what was acceptable behaviour and what wasn't. It was a grounding he took to heart.

"Damon was never much trouble and I knew he would be able to handle just about anything he had to," says Washington. "He is so dedicated and his desire is so great that I don't think he would do anything to jeopardize the goal he's had for so long."

The doubters in the crowd were many, and Stoudamire knew that once again he'd have to set the naysayers straight. He had done it from the time he was a child, when coaches, opponents and enemies told him he'd never make it to the NBA.

Draft night had arrived. And so had Damon Stoudamire.

GROWING UP

FEW EXPERIENCES LOOM LARGER in an eight-year-old's life than playing in a championship sporting event. On the playground, in the youth leagues, in the school system, winning a championship can establish credentials, create envy among peers and bring all sorts of recognition. Winners, even at that tender age, are treated differently. They have a different aura about them. They are given a wide berth on the courts, the football fields and the baseball diamonds. Reputations can be made, even at eight, that live through the teenage years and bring with them the key perks of adolescence.

So when Portland's Holy Redeemer School took to the court to battle for the city basketball championship back in 1982, Damon Stoudamire was ready to send a message.

"I was in the third grade, playing on a fifth-grade team. I was the best guy on the team, and we were playing for the city championship," he recalls matter-of-factly, the memory of something that occurred fifteen years ago coming back as if it happened yesterday.

"Now, this was when you were really young so they only kept score in the book, they didn't put it up on the board, so you didn't know what the score was during the game. I knew we were down by a lot but we were coming back and I was kicking some butt. And then the game ends and the other team starts jumping up and down. We lost — I don't know how much we lost by — and I was mad as hell.

"I went over there and I kicked the bench. I kicked it again, I tipped it over, and everybody was like, 'C'mon Damon, it's okay. It's only a game.'

"I was like, 'No way, man, we lost. That sucks!' I was crying and everything and it hurt. Right then, I knew losing was the worst feeling in the world. It's something I can't tolerate."

Charles Stoudamire, Damon's uncle and coach, took this opportunity to tell his eight-year-old nephew that outbursts rarely get people very far in life. It was a conversation Damon would never forget. The tenacity and desire to conquer that would manifest itself as he grew came early to Damon Stoudamire.

"I think Damon always knew he was going to be a

ballplayer," recalls his mother. "He liked competing against the other boys all the time in any sport. He was always younger than the people he played against so it was always a challenge, but I think he knew that's what he wanted to do at an early age.

"Damon was actually reading a newspaper before he was reading a schoolbook," she continues. "He would be at his grandmother's house, lying on the floor on his knees, and he'd be looking at the sports page. He couldn't have been more than four or five years old. I assumed he was looking at the pictures, but he'd be concentrating on the stats, too. Then he would listen to Howard Cosell and the other sports announcers and he could co-ordinate what he heard with what was in the newspapers — who was winning in what league and who the best players were. He'd pay attention to stats, to what the players were doing, and he'd always tell me he was going to do better, score more points, get more hits, score more touchdowns."

He was sowing the seeds of a winning-is-everything, I-want-to-be-the-best philosophy that has marked every step of his progress as a man and as an athlete.

"I don't know if I was reading, or what, but I knew what was going on," says Damon. In those days, he worshipped the NFL's Dallas Cowboys (and he still does). The Phoenix Suns were his favourite basketball team: Dennis Johnson, Walter Davis — those were his boys. Tiny Archibald, one of the smallest and smartest players in the league back then, was another who caught his eye. George Gervin was a favourite, too, primarily because he was among the most prolific scorers of the day; he was the "Ice Man," the cool guy who could fill up the basket. Damon knew that names at the top of the stats list were the names remembered.

"The guys who scored, those were the guys I wanted to be like." How much?

"We had these phone-in score-lines for sports. I don't know if they had them up in Canada, but they had the scores from every sport when it was in season. You could get updated on all the games, all the scores, all the time, every night. I used to call it so many times my mother had to cut out those numbers on the phone, 'cause I was killing the bills. I was calling every ten minutes. I had to know the scores, know who was scoring. It was how I kept up with the stats."

The early years of Stoudamire's life weren't all championship games and fun on the basketball court. Like hundreds of thousands of other young American children, he spent much of his childhood in a one-parent family. Willie Stoudamire and Liz Washington never married, and Willie left before his son was old enough to understand. Job opportunities for black men in Portland were few and far between, and when Willie was offered a job in Milwaukee, Wisconson, he decided to accept. "As I look back on the situation," Willie comments, "I realize that I didn't weigh all the things I should have from the standpoint of my family. I didn't understand the effect my leaving would have on them, and still does to this day." Nevertheless, there were some strong male figures in Damon's life: Willie's two brothers, Charles and Anthony, not only coached him in athletics, but also acted as important role models, while the father of Erin Cowan, Damon's best friend, treated Damon as part of the family. But it was his mom who had to handle much of the day-to-day raising of a child.

"The first two years after Willie left were a little shaky. It certainly wasn't the best situation for Damon, or for me," recalls Liz. Her own family was back in Las Vegas, and she had few close friends in Portland. It was hard to afford trips to Nevada each year, so it was pretty much Liz and Damon on their own.

"I guess I was pretty confident, even though I struggled and had to work a lot of overtime to help make ends meet. I don't know if Damon knows that sometimes there was a struggle. Sometimes kids aren't aware. But he had food on the table, nice clothes. Sometimes this bill didn't get paid right on time, sometimes that bill got put off, but we made out all right."

Damon never did want for much as a young boy. His singled-minded fascination with professional sports — especially his beloved Dallas Cowboys — made him easy to please at Christmas and on birthdays. "Damon always knew what he was going to get for Christmas — it would be some sports item or some clothing, always a sports team, almost always Dallas. He'd get the J. C. Penney catalogue out and he'd go through it and mark everything he wanted. Now, he wouldn't get every-thing. I'd go through and eliminate some of the stuff he had marked. But it seemed like every year was the same — a Cowboys shirt, maybe UNLV or Arizona. Everything had to be about sports."

Liz never had to worry about a sloppy-looking son, though. She can remember having to do load after load of laundry to keep up with her son's desire to be perfectly and neatly dressed every time he ventured out of the house. Damon claims he got this habit from his dad, who is also a neat freak.

"Damon would not wear his clothes twice. They always had to be pressed and cleaned. I couldn't even sneak a pair of pants past him, or a shirt. I had to be at work at seven and there wasn't much time in the morning, so I would lay out his clothes before we went to bed and he always had to be sure they were clean. If they weren't, he'd let me know, that's for sure."

And when he was stepping out, he was stepping out in style. Graduating from grade six might not be one of life's big moments for many of us, but it certainly was to a young Damon Stoudamire.

"I bugged my mom and bugged her and I got a tux to wear

to the graduation," he said. "I wanted a limo but she said no. I thought I was the man, though. Walking over to that school, seeing all the girls go *ooh, ahh*. I was strutting."

Liz, having learned to expect the unexpected from her son, took the tuxedo request in stride. The limo? That was another matter.

"Grade six, a tux, do you believe that?" says Liz. "I've got that picture and I laugh every time I look at it. The neighbours, they couldn't believe it, Damon in a tux to graduate grade school. Can you imagine if he'd had the limo? The people were talking about him for the tux, they would have never stopped talking if a big car had pulled up."

"That would have been something," Damon agrees. "The limo would have been the final piece."

For a youngster, the struggles of his parents are often the furthest thing from his mind. Paying bills, getting groceries, dealing with the day-to-day problems that arise in any family are not something a young teenager concerns himself with. Damon knew when he got home there would be a meal, and when he got up his clothes would be pressed and waiting for him. There might not have been a dad in the home, but there was most definitely a family.

"I guess it was tough, but at the same time, some people thought I was spoiled because of some of the stuff I had," is how Stoudamire recalls his adolescent years. "But I knew my mom was having a tough time sometimes. I used to always try to keep my stuff neat because I knew I wasn't going to get a whole lot."

Damon had little interest in the mundane life of a student, preferring to spend as much time as he possibly could on the basketball courts and baseball fields. It created some interesting challenges for his mom, who wanted to make sure there was some balance in her son's life.

"When Damon was in about the third grade, the teachers said they might want to put him in a special sort of class, one for kids who weren't slow but who were taking time to develop. I always thought if we had labelled him 'can't read' and put him in a special class, maybe it would have got imbedded in his mind that he couldn't read and he wouldn't have got better at it," recalls his mother. "I didn't want him to get branded, I knew that wouldn't do any good. So I listened to the teacher but I just worked with him myself, and he got along okay."

Because she had to leave for work at 7:00 a.m., every school day Liz Washington would wake Damon up and get him on his way to the home of his paternal grandmother, Wanda Stoudamire Matthews, which was just a ten-minute walk away. He'd have his breakfast there, and then take a nap, before walking across the street to school. He spent a lot of his time at his grandmother's when Liz was at work. Her house was something of a refuge for the young boy, and a place where Liz knew he would get the same love and nurturing he got at home. Damon knew it was a place he would be appreciated, and he loved the fact that his aunts and uncles and cousins gathered there on a regular basis. It was a place where he could find a friend whenever he thought his mom was being unreasonable. Getting in trouble is much less a big deal if there's an ally to run to.

"I'd tell my mom, 'I'm gonna call the children's authority, they're gonna take me away from you,'" he recalls of those days when he'd go scurrying to Grandma, hoping she'd take his side in some battle.

"My mom didn't beat me a lot but I used to get a whipping every now and then," says Damon, who has never for a minute blamed his mother for the punishment she doled out.

"I remember I got one when I was twelve after I stole a dollar from my grandma for PacMan — I was a PacMan addict, four quarters would last me a whole day — boy, did I get it that time. But she used to talk to me, too. She'd tell me what I did was wrong and why it was wrong." Damon attributes much of his characteristic self-discipline to his grandmother's influence.

If his mom wanted him home at a certain time and he thought he should be allowed to stay out later, or if his mom wanted him to spend more time on his homework than he thought was necessary, he might get ticked off and turn to his grandmother for help.

Liz, whose own father died when she was sixteen, listened to the advice of her mother-in-law, especially where Damon was concerned.

"She really helped us a lot. We'd get into an argument and Damon would go running over there, that's where he'd always go. I guess the last whipping with a belt I gave him was in the seventh or eighth grade. After that one, she sat me down one night and said Damon might be getting too old for that, maybe I had to try something else with him. I think she helped keep us close because I don't think Damon ever wanted to stay mad at me and I never wanted to stay mad at him. She was like the referee, and she helped us both."

Across the street from Damon's grandmother's house was Albina Park, a playground like the thousands of others in every city in the United States where dreams of NBA careers are born. There were a couple of basketball courts, tattered nets hanging from often bent rims with faded paint outlining the court on the cement. There was also a baseball diamond, and the usual playground equipment. It was a meeting place as much as a centre for sports.

In the playground culture of American inner cities, only the tough thrive and Portland was no different. Games of two-on-two, three-on-three, five-on-five are battles not only of basketball skill but of mental toughness. There are always teams waiting on the sidelines to challenge the winners, ready to knock off the best and ascend to the top, where bragging rights were to be had, where the top dogs ruled.

Because his talent made him stand out from the other kids his own age, Damon was always the youngest player in the game. And, invariably, he was the shortest, too. He had to overcome those challenges every time he took to the court, and he did it by developing his remarkable skills. In no time, word spread like wildfire about the uniquely skilled young boy who had some sort of aura about him.

"Guys would say, 'Damon, you got the game, you're going to the league,'" recalls Erin Cowan, who grew up with Damon and played with him every day on those playground courts. "We could all see it really early. We could all play a little ball, but Damon, he was the most dedicated. He worked hard every day. He just had a different approach. And a little more talent," he understates.

When Stoudamire was eight years old, he had to beat back challenges from ten-year-olds. When he was ten, the twelve-year-olds would try and knock him off. Every day was a new challenge; every day was proving time again.

This playground proving ground is something difficult for young Canadians to understand. The structured world of minor hockey — which starts with house leagues and moves up to rep hockey to junior B to junior A or American colleges and finally to a professional league — bears no resemblance to the free-form development of basketball in the United States. Sure, there are summer camps and school leagues and club systems available to some, but most kids practise on the black-tops of schoolyards and playgrounds. They learn to play hard and battle every day and win every game; losers are banished to the sidelines to watch until their turn comes around again.

It's the kind of system that fosters a level of intensity and hunger for success that separates the suspects from the prospects and instils a killer instinct in someone as young as eight. It teaches him that losing "sucks." It gives him the rage to kick over a bench and get angry at those who would console him. It sows the seeds of a winner.

Damon's father, Willie, who played basketball at Portland State University and was selected by the Seattle Supersonics in the eighth round of the 1972 NBA draft, was something of a local legend, and his reputation was there for his son to try to emulate. Willie's brother Charles coached Damon's basketball team and was drafted by the NFL Detroit Lions; his brother Anthony coached Damon's youth football team and played quarterback for Portland State University. Not surprisingly, the name Stoudamire carried some cachet on the streets of Portland, where Charles and Anthony and Willie were well known as excellent athletes.

"I think it might have been tough for him," says Isiah Thomas. "His dad was a high-profile guy in the community and in the playgrounds, and Damon had a high profile, too. He had some living up to do."

"Yeah, people knew who he was and they knew I was his son," says Damon, "but I don't think it made it any tougher. I don't think my name made me what I am. I just played."

Willie might not have lived with Damon and Liz, but perhaps it was from his dad that Damon got the gift of athletic talent. If you can talk about a "natural" in a game that takes years and years of practice and hard work to master, Damon Stoudamire is it. He was no Tiger Woods, driven incessantly by his father to a level incomprehensible to a grade-school boy; he wasn't like some teenage tennis prodigy relentlessly banging balls back across a net until burnout and the physical wear and tear render him a has-been by the time he's ready for the senior prom. Damon Stoudamire was just a young kid who wanted to play ball. Any kind of ball.

"I was probably a better baseball player than I was a basketball player when I was really young, but I loved basketball and I didn't love baseball. I knew I could skip a baseball game to go play basketball," he recalls. And he knows exactly the moment that hit home.

"I was thirteen years old. We had won state in basketball and we were about to go to the nationals, and we were about to go to state in baseball," he recalls. Both teams needed him and wanted him because, without his skills, their chances of success were significantly diminished. In fact, in the baseball tournament leading to the state finals, he had pitched a couple of no-hitters. His team would have to lose two successive games to be eliminated, and that possibility was remote if Stoudamire played.

He didn't.

"I left that morning for basketball," Damon says. "We lost both those baseball games and I knew right then I loved basketball more. I could leave baseball but only to go to basketball."

Despite shifting his attention to basketball, Damon was a good enough baseball prospect as a pitcher and centre-fielder to attract some attention from major league scouts. He could pitch and he could run and he could catch a baseball with the best of them, but something clicked the first time he picked up a basketball. It's a feeling that can't be described adequately by someone who doesn't possess the tremendous amount of natural ability all NBA players initially display. It's just a sense, and the greats all know it.

"When I first started playing, when I was able to pick up a basketball, I knew I wanted to be a player," recalls Damon. "I would play all the time. I would work on my game back then, and I knew I would do it."

Finding a place to develop that game was Stoudamire's biggest obstacle. Unlike New York, with its infamous inner-city playgrounds that have served as a training ground for any number of great players, or Chicago, where cut-throat games in the projects and on the high school courts build players with an edge to their games and their personalities, or any of the warm-weather cities where games can be played outdoors 365 days a year, or even the hoops-crazed areas like Indiana and Charlotte, North Carolina, Portland is hardly considered a hotbed of basketball.

The self-styled "City That Works" is home to 1.6 million people, many employed by upscale industries. High-tech manufacturers like Intel, NEC, Toshiba, Epson and Fujitsu create the city's wealth. Nestled in the confluence of the Willamette and Columbia rivers, Portland is a major centre of commerce, industry, transportation, finance and distribution for the Pacific northwest, one hundred miles from the Pacific Ocean, with the spectre of the Cascade Mountains looming in the east. In the trendy cafés along the downtown waterfront, locals sip the white wines and wheat beers the city is famous for while the peaks of Mt. Jefferson, Mt. Hood, Mt. Adams, Mt. Rainier and the still-smouldering Mt. St. Helens stand sentry in the distance.

The family home on 9th Street was pretty typical, although it was likely cleaner and neater than most. Damon always did the chores his mom asked him to do, and he did them without complaint. Theirs was a typical middle-class neighbourhood outside the downtown area. And while Portland was a pretty sleepy city by comparison with New York, Chicago or Los Angeles, like any American city, it had its share of gang activity. A few blocks away was a different world, where drugs and petty thievery presented the potential for trouble.

Damon stayed out of it, and for the most part, the teens hanging around the corners knew to leave the little guy and his friends alone. As long as there was Irving Park, the Dishman Recreation Centre, a basketball and a group of his buddies, Damon would be okay. He didn't want to get mixed up with the gangs; he knew that wasn't the way to go about reaching his goals. Besides, it looked like a boring life, standing around just hanging. He would rather have been on the courts or in the field playing ball.

"If you went a block or two, it was bad, and we all knew it, Damon especially," says Erin Cowan, who grew up just a few blocks from Damon and Liz. "But we had each other, we all had strong parents, and Damon knew what he wanted to do. We were ballplayers, we really didn't bother with the negative influences or let them get to us. They were there, but Damon knew that stuff didn't lead anywhere good."

And the kids who didn't have his desire didn't press him to join a gang or give up his games. Maybe they figured it wasn't worth the effort; maybe they saw something in him that told them he had a promising future. For whatever reasons, he didn't get dragged down.

"It was a tough neighbourhood, there were some tough people, but for the most part nobody messed with me. I was always referred to as a 'hooper.' The guys saw that was what I wanted to do and they pretty much left me to do it. No one messed with me, no one tried to get me to go bad," says Stoudamire. "They had gangs and all that but I never really got into that. It wasn't something I wanted to do."

It was tough to display that strength of will, but Damon and Erin, Damon's cousin Antoine and a couple of other buddies managed it. It wasn't, however, that they were never close to trouble.

"I remember I was at a party and a guy got caught with some buckshot. Someone just shot and got this guy in the side of the face, there was blood everywhere," he recalls. "I got the hell out of there in a hurry — it was wild, and I ran. I knew the only thing that could catch me was a bullet."

Gang violence in Portland might not be as prominent to casual observers as it is in bigger cities, but it does exist, and Damon saw it up close.

"I've been in the park where they had some straight shootouts, guys just shooting. I'd run, man, bob and weave, hit the ground and get out of there as quick as I could. That wasn't my scene and I didn't belong there."

Damon's mother, too, was conscious of the dangers that her teenage son was facing. Liz felt secure in the way she was raising young Damon, secure he knew right from wrong, good from bad, but still, as she sat at her desk at work, she wondered. And worried.

"When he was growing up, I guess he was a typical kid," she says now. "I had my problems with him. I don't think any mother doesn't have some problems with her child. But now that he's older and he's doing what he's doing, I look back and he wasn't that bad, considering some of the other kids and what they're doing today.

"The worst problem I ever had with him was curfew. The guys he hung out with were about two years older than him. His cousin Antoine was two years older too, and he used to spend a lot of time with him and his friends.

"I guess the best way to put it was Damon was always more mature than the kids in his own age group, so he never spent a lot of time with them. The kids he was hanging out with got to stay out for an hour or two later than I wanted Damon to. We had some battles over that."

She needn't have worried. He might have been out late but he was staying out of trouble.

"Yeah, I had a problem with coming home late. It was a big problem, probably the biggest problem I had," he says. "I always hung out with older people and I didn't want to be the

HAVING A BALL: At one year old, Damon goes for a stroll around his neighbourhood, trusty ball in hand. It certainly wasn't the last time he left home ready to play ball.

Liz Washington collection

TAKING A WALK: At eight months old, Damon took his first steps. Notice how he looks like he's ready to play defence.

Liz Washington collection

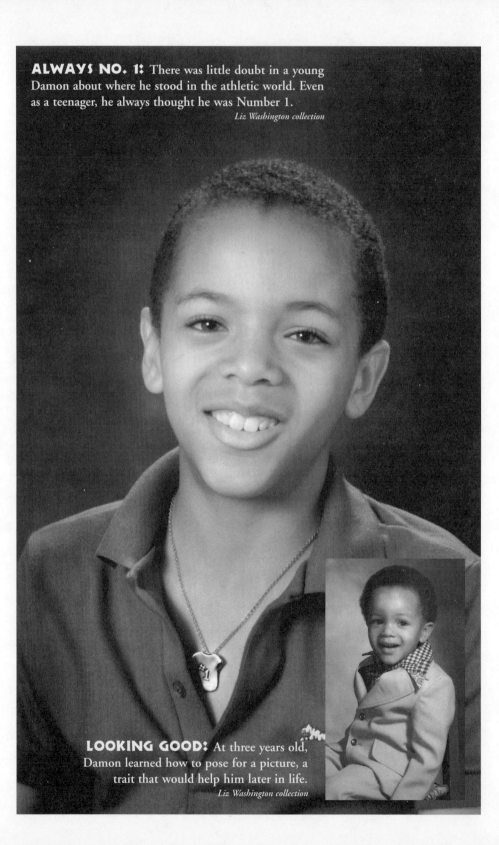

ALWAYS NO. 1: There was little doubt in a young Damon about where he stood in the athletic world. Even as a teenager, he always thought he was Number 1.

Liz Washington collection

LOOKING GOOD: At three years old, Damon learned how to pose for a picture, a trait that would help him later in life.

Liz Washington collection

MOTHER AND SON: Strong family values are as much a part of Damon's personality as his athletic prowess. They were instilled by his mom, Liz Washington, who made the sacrifices of a single parent to raise her only son.

Liz Washington collection

CAUGHT IN THE MIDDLE: Damon was a huge sports fan growing up and he wore his allegiances proudly. He's a big Dallas Cowboy fan to this day, shunting aside, apparently, the Raiders.

Liz Washington collection

STYLIN': Steppin' out to graduate grade school the first time he ever put on a tuxedo. Damon wanted a limousine, too, but Liz thought that might just be too much.

Liz Washington collection

STEPPING TO THE PLATE:

Damon was a good enough baseball player as a teenager to attract some attention from scouts. However, he learned at about 13 that he could leave baseball behind to concentrate on his first love, basketball.

WITH THE DOCTOR:

Jack Ramsay is a basketball legend in Portland, having led the Trail Blazers to an NBA title. His basketball camp each summer was the place to be for up and coming young players like Damon.

Liz Washington collection

READY FOR ACTION:

Basketball wasn't the only sport Damon was interested in as a youth. He donned the football gear one Christmas morning, perhaps thinking about a future with his beloved Cowboys.

STAR AMONG STARS: The 1996 NBA rookie all-star game was Damon's big breakthrough on a league-wide stage. He soared through the air and came away with the most valuable player honours in the showcase event.

NBA Photo/Andy Hayt

LAYING IT UP: Holding off a member of the Philadelphia 76ers, Damon delivers one of his patented layups during a 1997 game.

NBA Photos/Nathaniel S. Butler

GIVING SOME ADVICE: Damon is always in huge demand. Here he answers questions for a couple of teenagers before a game as part of an interview for an NBA magazine.

NBA Photos/Ron Turenne

STRETCHING OUT: The physical demands of an NBA game mean it's imperative every muscle is ready for action. Damon spends about 20 minutes before each game stretching out on the court.

NBA Photos/Barry Gossage

ELEVATING HIS GAME: Damon takes off over Charles Barkley and the Houston Rockets. Established stars like Barkley and Jordan have developed a healthy respect for the young Stoudamire.

NBA Photo/Bill Baptist

IN HIGH DEMAND:

The trappings of super-stardom include signing an awful lot of auto-graphs, at the games and on the streets. Damon is often stopped and asked to sign whatever piece of paper may be handy.

NBA Photos/Ron Turenne

FAMILY CELEBRATION: Damon's mom, Liz Washington, and his dad, Willie Stoudamire, were on hand the day he signed his first contract. Each was equally proud of their only child.

NBA Photos

PUPIL AND THE TEACHER: Isiah Thomas took some heat when he used the first draft pick in Raptors history on a small point guard from Arizona. But on the day Damon signed his first contract, there were smiles all around.

NBA Photos

one to say, 'Y'all got to take me home, my mother wants me home at twelve midnight,' when they could stay out as long as they wanted. I guess I thought you just gotta hang and take it later from your mom.

"I used to creep through the screen door, take off my shoes before I got in the house the whole way and try to tiptoe right into my bedroom. Sometimes she'd catch me, sometimes she didn't."

And if she did?

"She'd give it to me good."

Erin remembers time after time when Damon would drag himself home at 2:00 a.m. instead of midnight. Even though Liz trusted Damon, Erin and the other guys in the small, close-knit circle, everyone knew there would be hell to pay.

"We'd get Damon home at 2:00 a.m. on a Saturday night and he'd call me Sunday and say, 'Hey, I gotta stay in for the next couple of nights. I'll see you Monday or Tuesday.' We knew he was in trouble, but we knew he'd be back. And we knew he'd be out late again pretty soon. But you know what it's like, it's five to 12:00, he says he's got to be home at 12:00 and we're fifteen minutes from his place. We'd say, 'Hang in, we'll leave in ten minutes,' but then it'd be 12:30 or 1:00 so we just stayed out. He'd say, 'If I'm going to get in trouble, it might as well be worth it.' So we'd go home at 2:00 a.m."

Damon had one brush with trouble as a high school

student, a moment he will never forget and one he never wants to relive. It taught him how vulnerable athletes are to criticism, and how enemies will use anything to unnerve even a teenage prodigy.

The incident in question was a lunch-hour food fight at Wilson High School. The innocent prank turned ugly when the food being tossed around was quickly replaced by punches after someone took unkindly to getting hit. Even though Damon played a minor role in the fracas, the police were eventually called and he was charged with second-degree assault. The charges were later dropped, but Damon's reputation was tarnished. It didn't take long for him to suffer the barbs of opposing players and their fans. That's what hurt the most.

"When I came back to play, it was real bad. I was just playing, but they were calling me stuff like 'jailbird,' and my mom and dad were in the gym. That really hurt, because people didn't understand what had happened, things just got out of control. They thought I was a bad person. They thought I was a criminal. That's when I knew I had to keep clean — cleaner than everyone else."

Being raised by one parent has given Damon some definite ideas about how he would raise a family of his own. He can remember the financial burden his mother bore to ensure he had everything he needed, and how that made him feel.

"When you don't have any money, you're always thinking about how to get some. Man, there would be times when my pockets would be leaking. Now, my uncles would get me some chump change, just walkin' around money, and my mother was always there for me, but I never had a lot, that's for sure.

"And there's nothing like having leaking pockets when the people around you have money. That's tough, and I know how that feels. My mom, she never left me flat broke, but there sure wasn't much to go around.

"I've always said, 'When I get some money, I'm going to take care of it. And if I have a kid, I'm going to take care of him.'"

Willie Stoudamire returned to Portland when Damon was a freshman in high school. Damon's grandmother died about six months later, and the whole family felt the loss. Wanda Stoudamire Matthews had been the glue that kept everyone together.

Willie worked hard at re-establishing his relationship with his son. Having been away for many years, it wasn't easy for him to earn Damon's trust. But over the past decade, that process has been solidified, and Willie now acts as Damon's business manager for the myriad off-court endorsement opportunities that come his son's way.

The re-emergence of his father as a strong influence has created a difficult situation for Damon. His parents are not close, and since his grandmother passed away, Damon is their only common bond.

"My mom and I are definitely not as close as we used to be," Damon says. "There's been a lot of tension between her and my father, and now I'm stuck in the middle, and that takes its toll on me. I want to keep the relationships the same, the one with my mom and the one with my dad, but it's hard.

"He was gone for ten years, and my mother never asked him for a single cent of child support. I can count on the fingers of two hands the times he sent stuff to help us out. That will break a person's heart, and it's hard to forget it all."

Willie's business skills have provided Damon with someone to help him sift through the offers he gets and take care of things away from the basketball court. The friction that exists between his mother and father will always exist but Damon's trying to keep both as part of his inner circle, and that means treating both parents with tact and respect.

"Even if my mom doesn't understand a lot about business, I still want her informed on things that are going on," Damon says. "My mom wonders why he didn't want to be around for those other years. To this day, I honestly think he left and came back and didn't think he did anything wrong. He thought that was just a choice he made, and I don't think he realizes just what that choice meant to me or my mom. I let him know, though."

Liz Washington knows, however, that Damon appreciates the sacrifices she made when he was growing up and what their relationship is and always will be. It's tough to see Willie back in Damon's life on such a scale, but she's secure enough to know there will always be room for her.

"I'm the kind of person to sit in the back seat and not make a big fuss," she says, her voice beginning to show emotion. "I know what Damon's going through. There's a lot of pressure on him in his basketball life and in his private life, and he doesn't need to have me bickering with Willie all the time.

"There are a lot of bad feelings there. I raised Damon on my own — financially and every way — and I get very emotional about it.

"Damon knows how I feel, though, and I know how he feels about me."

GETTING A GAME

EVERYTHING HAPPENS QUICKLY on an NBA court — much more quickly than the people sitting in the stands or in their homes watching on television can relate to. The players are giants — six-foot-six, six-foot-eight, seven feet tall — but they are not plodding behemoths, thinking before each step. They are finely tuned athletes, arguably the best athletes in any sport anywhere in the world. The pace of the game is lightning quick, the collisions are jarring, and they play the game above the ground and above the ten-foot basket. Long gone are the days of methodical offences, with four or five passes and deliberate movements away from the ball designed to free up a forward for a set shot or create a nice layup for the guards. It's an instinctive game now, the result of hours and hours and days and days and years and years of practice that have honed the intuitive skills of its best players. Sometimes it's just a look between a guard and a forward that results in one of those highlight-reel alley-oop plays. Sometimes it's the end result of years of two players working together on the same team that results in a no-look pass setting up a thunderous dunk. It is a game of action and reaction more than anything else. Its motto should be "Don't think. Just play."

There is no position on a basketball court that requires the kind of pure instinct that the point guard spot does. In fact, there may be no other position in all of sports that requires such an incredibly demanding combination of athletic ability and split-second judgment in the cauldron of competition. The football quarterback probably comes the closest, but when he hands the ball off, it never comes back to him; his team's success is as dependent on the defence as it is on anything he does. A baseball pitcher does little more than put the ball in play; others determine the outcome of the action he generates. Soccer may be as full of motion as basketball, but there is no one player who dictates the pace of action or the possession of the ball. Hockey is as fluid a game as basketball, yet no single skater dominates possession of the puck and dictates the outcome of each offensive set in the way that the point guard does.

Amid the screams from the crowd, exhortations from the

team bench and chatter from the different players going to their assigned places on the court, the point guard must make the right move, or everything breaks down. He has to dissect what his four teammates are doing, what his five opponents are doing, what his coach wants him to do and what the referee is likely to do. He has to know the game situation, the shot-clock situation, which of his teammates is having a hot night and which might be able to expose a defensive liability in his opponent. He has to know which of his teammates like the ball up high, which like it down low, which shooter likes to get the ball after he has set himself up, which shooter wants to take a couple of dribbles before taking a shot. Is the man defending him too quick to be beaten off the dribble? Is he slow enough that a couple of head fakes and maybe a step to the left will create a clean opportunity for a 3-point field goal attempt? Once the point guard passes the ball, he has to know where to go on the floor. Should he slash to the basket looking for the return pass or hit a point on the perimeter in order to receive the ball in a prime shooting location? There are a lot of things going through a point guard's mind.

"It's just basketball smarts, I don't know any other way to describe it," says Stoudamire. "At this level, you just know what to do. At least, the good ones know what to do."

It takes years and years to develop basketball smarts. They don't come from a coach drawing plays on a blackboard or drilling them into his players' heads; they don't come from sitting in front of television screens watching videos until your eyes blur. They come from playing the game — in public school, in the playgrounds, in high school, again and again. They come from playing in college and in summer leagues. The apparently instinctive moves of a Damon Stoudamire in a no-look pass to Marcus Camby, the one-handed bounce pass to Doug Christie on the break, the shovel pass to a wide-open Walt Williams for a 3-pointer — they come from hard, hard work. For Damon, who is listed at five-foot-ten (he'll admit in a moment of weakness to actually being five-foot-nine in bare feet, but an inch here or there at that height is nothing to quibble about), that hard work includes convincing sceptical coaches, teammates and opponents that you've got what it takes.

By the time Damon Stoudamire reached Wilson High School in Portland in 1987, his reputation as a budding basketball star was on its way to being made. In the summer-time AAU and recreation centre games, he was tagged as a small boy with a big game. On the playgrounds, he and his buddies were known as the up-and-comers, the next high school legends. Damon had been to basketball camp each summer for years and years, and those camps had helped develop his game. In Portland, there might not be a more famous basketball name than Jack Ramsay, who led Bill Walton, Maurice Lucas, Lionel Hollins, Dave Twardzik and the rest of the Trail Blazers to the 1976–77 championship — still, perhaps, the greatest moment in Portland sports history. Ramsay, now a highly respected television analyst of NBA games, took a liking to the small but determined young Stoudamire. As a coach, he was enamoured of players with intelligence, players who could think their way through situations, pass the ball and play sound basketball. Stoudamire says he grew up idolizing the likes of high-scoring ABA and NBA star George Gervin and the little and talented Tiny Archibald, but seeing the Trail Blazers in their home town gave him an appreciation for the smart, simple game.

When you're the smallest kid around, you have to be able to throw the right pass, dribble like a demon, defend with a tenacity that belies your physical limitations. Because he studied the game, its intricacies and all the players, Stoudamire knew he had to create a solid foundation on which to build his skills. If he couldn't master the basics of dribbling, shooting or passing, he would never make it.

"I guess I had to work hard, but it really wasn't work. At least I didn't think of it that way. Because if you play ball long enough and you've got any kind of skill to start with, you're going to get good."

As soon as Stoudamire started to make his mark in the NBA, the chroniclers wanted to know about that hard work, about how the lightning-fast ball of dynamite came to possess such astounding skills. They trekked to Wilson High School, where they sought out friends and foes, coaches and family members, to find out just how he came to be. They found a willing commentator in Dick Beachell, the high school coach who helped start Stoudamire on his path to fame and greatness.

"Tell Damon he can't do something and he'll stick it right back in your face," is Beachell's strongest recollection of his star. "You will never meet a more mentally tough individual than Damon."

Beachell knew Damon would never give up, because he did something very few coaches have ever done.

Erin Cowan recalls the first game Stoudamire was to play for Wilson, a school about 10 miles from his home. Damon had chosen the school for its athletic excellence and because it was far enough from the neighbourhood where he grew up that he wouldn't be tempted to just hang around with the guys. That day, the little sophomore didn't play. He was nailed to the bench and never saw a minute of action. For someone who was a playground legend and known throughout Portland, someone who had been around all the great high school players for years, it was a slap in the face. He might only have been barely over five feet tall, but he knew he could play, and that's what he wanted to do. "He was mad, really mad," recalls Cowan. "He told me he had never sat out a whole game before in his life, not in AAU ball, not at the rec centre, nowhere. He was so mad he wanted to transfer."

Damon vowed it wouldn't happen a second time. And it didn't. "I don't know if it made me work harder, because I was working hard all the time," he said. "It wasn't so much of an insult, but it hurt, because I knew I could play and I knew they'd realize it soon enough."

What Stoudamire did was become the best basketball player Wilson ever produced, leading the school to two state championships in three years and helping it to a phenomenal record of 74–4 during his career. He averaged a stunning 26 points, 9 assists and 3.6 rebounds a game as a senior. Then he capped his high school career by being named the Oregon player of the year and earning recognition from Converse as a high school All-American. He might not have started his first game, but he never looked back from that moment on.

"He did so much for our program, I've not seen one like him before or since," said Beachell. "The one overriding factor behind how good he was, and how good he is, is how hard he works. Damon never, ever slacks off. He just has a real desire to succeed.

"I remember the first time I saw him. He couldn't have been more than five feet tall and about 120 pounds dripping wet. It wasn't the physical dimensions that set Damon apart, though.

You could tell he was cocky and he could back it up. He was clever, he was smart, and he knew what he wanted to do."

Liz Washington had listened to her son recite chapter and verse about NBA players practically from the time he could speak, and she had listened to him tell everyone within earshot that some day he would play in the league. She knew, however, that a journey from the playgrounds and high schools of Portland to the bright lights of the NBA doesn't come from dreams and idle talk. Anyone who watched him play knew he had a game that would take him places, but she knew there were other standards to achieve as well. A college scholarship would soon be in the offing, and while Damon was bright — about an average student, he says — hitting the books didn't hold nearly as much allure as hitting a jump shot.

"I knew Damon had the desire to play in the pros and go to college first. There were times when his grades would drop and I'd tell him they weren't going to let him play with bad grades, they'd pull him off the team," she recalls. "He'd tell me he didn't care, but I'd say 'You've worked this hard and come this far and you're going to maybe give it all up because of your school grades.' I wasn't pushing him, I was just letting him know the consequences.

"I remember at Wilson there was this counsellor for the minority students. He called me one day and I went down to the school. He said he knew Damon was doing okay at basketball, and he knew that Damon's dad was a basketball player and he probably wanted to be just like his dad. Then he said with Damon's height, his chance of even getting a Division 1 scholarship were slim, and that he and I should be prepared to face reality. Now, I listened, but all I could do was laugh inside because this guy obviously didn't know Damon too well. I don't think he realized how good a basketball player he was and how set he was on reaching his goals. When Damon sets his mind to something, he usually accomplishes it."

An undisputed star on the court, Damon would never light up a classroom like he did a basketball court. But the fact that he routinely pulled in Cs instead of As when the report cards were handed out didn't mean a thing to him. Aside from the education he was getting in the classroom, he was picking up "street smarts" in everyday life. The combination of the two gave him a well-rounded experience that would carry him through to adulthood.

His propensity for doing just enough in high school followed him to college as well. After an intense recruitment battle, Damon accepted a basketball scholarship from the University of Arizona and by the fall of 1991, he was a college freshman. Although scholarship athletes are given wide berth, they still have to carry a substantial classroom workload. When Damon arrived in Tucson, he wasn't sure what the college course load would be like and, like hundreds of other freshman athletes, he found it hard to balance sports and school. It took a while for him to acclimate himself, a period that included one threat of academic probation, which would have made him ineligible for his first semester on the basketball team. That got his attention quickly.

"I must have changed my major two or three times before I finally liked what I did," Damon says of his first year at Arizona. In the end, he decided to major in media arts and minor in sports broadcasting, providing him with a background well suited for some job in media or perhaps entertainment when his athletic career ends.

"Here I am, going to college, and I didn't really know what I wanted to take. People are telling me what to take so I can just get by, and there I am in psychology and sociology, and I really didn't care about any of that. Now, Arizona's got like 47,000 or 48,000 students and it's like a city. No one gives a damn about most people, but I was a basketball player, so I could get all the help I needed. I got a tutor for all four years. She helped me so much, she was the person who made me want to do schoolwork. I hated schoolwork when I got there, but she knew how to get the best out of me. I wasn't the best at writing down my thoughts. I'd get distracted and I didn't want to do it, so she'd say, 'Just talk, tell me about it' and she'd be typing away, getting my thoughts down. She taught me how to study. I thought I knew how to study but I didn't know anything about it. She got me through, that's for sure."

He never needed tutors on the basketball court, though. The men who coached him at the recreation centre, at school and at the summer camps all use the same phrase to describe him — a student of the game. He took all they said, absorbed it and turned it into action on the floor. "You never had to tell him the same thing twice," says Beachell.

The college recruiting process is something with which young Canadian athletes are, for the most part, unfamiliar. It starts practically from before the time a kid reaches high school, when his talent in the playground brings out the bird-dogs and would-be agents trying to steer a player to a certain school. There are often payouts involved — under-the-table considerations if somebody can get a player to a particular school — all illegal but commonplace nonetheless. Because Damon had skills seldom seen in someone so young, he grabbed his fair share of attention. Oregon State coach Jim Anderson once said that one of his biggest regrets was not being able to keep his state's star at home. "I recruited him as hard as I possibly could. Not because I thought he might be a great player, but because I knew it. A lot of times, you'll see a little guard in high school and you don't visualize him having that kind of impact at a higher level," he said in a feature story before Stoudamire made his last appearance with the Arizona Wildcats against the Oregon Beavers. "But I always thought

Damon was a prospect because of his knowledge of the game, because of his talent and his work ethic, and because he has such a big, big heart."

Stoudamire figured a little guy with a big game and a bigger heart needed a big program to play for. Growing up, he'd split his college loyalties between the University of Nevada–Las Vegas and Arizona, depending primarily on which team was hot at the time. But the UNLV Runnin' Rebels were always running afoul of the NCAA rules, locking coach Jerry Tarkanian and the entire program into a long-running legal battle, and the future there was cloudy at best. Not so at Arizona, where Lute Olson's program was consistently among the best in the country, the Wildcats' style of play fit perfectly with Stoudamire's game, and the state was crazy for hoops. As a thirteen-year-old, playing at summer camp in Long Beach, California, against players three years older than him, Stoudamire caught Olson's eye. Not surprisingly, the legendary Wildcat coach first noticed Stoudamire because he was the smallest player in the league. But Olson was impressed with his brain, his quickness and his competitive nature — all the things everyone mentions when they talk about the young prodigy.

"Arizona was a good fit," says Stoudamire. "Basketball was huge there. I liked that. I was going to play right away, and it was just the right place for me to go."

Absolutely.

Stoudamire took the NCAA by storm. In his freshman year, he averaged more than 7 points and 2.5 assists per game. He was named to the Pac-10 conference freshman all-star team. In his sophomore year, he exerted himself even more, leading Arizona to a 17–1 record, being named to the conference all-star team and averaging 11 points, 5.7 assists and 4.6 rebounds a game. He spent the summer of 1993 picking up some valuable experience by leading the United States team to the gold medal at the World University Games in Buffalo. Coincidentally, in a dramatic gold-medal game, the team Stoudamire and the Americans beat was Canada.

Stoudamire's third season at Arizona was his breakthrough year, the season in which he gained national prominence on a level that he had been expecting from the time he first picked up a ball. The 1993–94 Wildcats had one of the best backcourts in the United States in Stoudamire and Khalid Reeves, and they carried Arizona all the way to the NCAA Final Four, where the Wildcats lost a tough semifinal to the eventual champions from Arkansas. Stoudamire's 27 points and 10 rebounds in the West regional final was one of the highlights of his young career and came on the heels of a regular season in which he'd averaged 18 points and 6 assists and was an Honourable Mention All-American.

After losing to East Tennessee State in the NCAA tournament

following his freshman year and losing as a number two seed to number fifteen Santa Clara after his sophomore season (one of the most stunning upsets in recent NCAA tournament history), that ride to the Final Four was an incredible journey. It more than made up for the first two years of post-season disappointment.

"At Arizona, it's like pro basketball. The Phoenix Suns are number 1 and we were 1A. Everybody talked about us and followed us. That Santa Clara loss was devastating, just devastating. When we lost that game, we got killed, and I don't think I've ever felt that bad."

The media spotlight was harsh on the Wildcats after that horrendous loss in a game everyone had expected them to win easily. Damon was castigated for his poor performance, which brought to a sudden end a season of great promise for Arizona.

"When we lost to Santa Clara, they ripped me bad. I was like 0 for 10. I only made about six free throws and I must have had seven turnovers. I was terrible. Khalid had a bad game, too, a real bad game. He was getting taken off the dribble by some surfer dude. It was ridiculous.

"That's when I learned how tough it would be. They said all kinds of bad stuff about me — that I was no good, that I choked in the big game — it was tough to take.

"The next year we went to the Final Four and, man, that was great. There was no feeling like being that kind of winner. The people loved us. You can't beat that feeling. Even when we lost, when we came back to Arizona they just about closed down the city. They drove us around in convertibles. They had three or four parties for us. I've never felt like that before or since. I had so much fun. That was the best year of my life, right there."

After such a stunning season, the pressure was on Stoudamire — as it is on all young players these days, it seems — to turn professional and forgo his final year of college eligibility. But, again showing poise and maturity beyond his years, he decided it would be best for his game if he remained at Arizona for another year and honed his skills even more.

During the summer, he was the captain of the American team at the Goodwill Games, a tournament in St. Petersburg, Russia, that attracted scouts from almost every NBA franchise. In fact, it was at that team's training camp in California that Isiah Thomas saw Stoudamire and became even more impressed with the kid's game than he had been after watching him on television.

Stoudamire enhanced his reputation exponentially during his senior season, after Reeves had gone to the NBA and he was left to carry the burden alone. He never missed a beat: he averaged 22.8 points and 7.3 assists per game, and he was named a consensus All-American in voting by the Associated Press, *Basketball Weekly*, the National Association of Basketball Coaches and the *Basketball Times*, and a finalist for college player of the year by voters for the James Naismith Award and the U.S. Basketball Writers group. He was also tied for Pac-10 player of the year, sharing the award with Ed O'Bannon of the UCLA Bruins, who had led his team to the NCAA championship. Damon finished his college career as the second player in conference history to have at least 1,800 points, 600 assists and, incredibly, 400 rebounds; he is Arizona's fourth leading all-time scorer, with 1,849 points, and the school's second leading assist-getter, with 663.

If Damon Stoudamire learned his game in Portland's Irving Park and in the Wilson High School gym, he perfected his game at Arizona. He was good when he got to college; he was great when he left.

"In four years of practice situations, Damon was always alert and competing," Lute Olson said. "There was never one case where he went through the motions. He's one of the most conscientious players I've ever coached and one of the hardest workers. The bottom line with Damon is that he knows the big picture and he's aiming for it. He can only change what he controls. Things he can't control won't bother him because he has that don't-worry approach."

Traditionally, the point guard has simply been the floor leader, the guy who brings the ball up court and passes it off to the scorers. It's been a creative position, filled by a man who starts things that others finish. But the position that once was the domain of the likes of Bob Cousy and Jerry West has evolved, and Stoudamire is ready to lead the evolution into the next millennium. When point guards were content to dribble outside the key and simply dish the ball off, it meant defenders could slack off because they didn't have to worry all the time about point guards getting near the basket. Stoudamire is one of a new breed, able to handle the scoring and also create different offensive opportunities for himself, through either drives to the basket or deadly outside shooting. Even at his size, his quickness makes it possible for him to get clear paths to the basket, paths he uses either to score himself or pass off to teammates when opposing defenders leave their men to come cover him.

And with the Raptors, the more he does, the better. There was a time in the middle of the second season when some so-called experts were questioning the number of shots he was taking, sending coach Darrell Walker into a fit of apoplexy. "Who else is going to shoot?" he asked between expletives one night in the bowels of the SkyDome. "What am I going to do, tell the best shooter we've got not to shoot? If he doesn't shoot, we don't score, and if we don't score, we don't win. Shoot too much? That's stupid."

That Stoudamire is a gunner, unafraid to put up the 3-

pointer at any time in the game, willing to take the shot with the game on the line, comes from years and years of being the go-to guy for his team. He might have a relatively low shooting percentage, but there are some legitimate reasons for that. In the Toronto offensive scheme, the ball is always in his hands when an offensive set breaks down and the 24-second shot clock is running out. Four or five times a night he has to put up desperation jumpers from some ungodly spot on the court, and seldom do they fall. Give him wide-open jumpers and the shooting percentage would soar.

In the past, point guards operated under a pass-first, shoot-second philosophy, but that's not the way the game is going these days. In fact, one of the players who accelerated the change towards scoring point guards was Isiah Thomas, when he was leading the Detroit Pistons from the bottom of the heap to a pair of NBA championships. Thomas gave those Detroit teams a double-edged attack by choosing either to score himself or pass the ball off to a teammate. When Magic Johnson first burst onto the scene in the early 1980s, he was thought to be the exception to the traditional short point guard, who was often the smallest player on the floor. At six-feet, nine inches, Johnson spent his entire career reinventing the position, combining a small point guard's ability to handle the ball with a big man's ability to get down low near the basket and muscle his way inside. Johnson, though, was the exception to the rule. There has never been, and likely won't ever be, another player like him, and the days of the six-foot-nine point guard are gone. Now, it's Damon Stoudamire and players like Philadelphia's Allen Iverson and Minnesota's Stephon Marbury — quick players well under six-foot-five — who will become the floor generals for the next decade. They all have the quick, slashing-shooting style that creates the buzz in the arenas and around the league.

Duels between Stoudamire and Iverson promise to be among the best in the NBA for the duration of their careers. At six-foot-three, Iverson is a bit taller but just as quick as Stoudamire. He was the rookie of the year in the season following Stoudamire's. He plays for the Philadelphia 76ers, guaranteeing four games a year against Stoudamire and the Raptors. When the two first hooked up in the 1996–97 season, it was like two heavyweights — perhaps welterweights might be a more apt description — feeling each other out. But there are flaws to Iverson's game that Stoudamire, because he's a smarter player, can expose. Even though their physical skills are similar, Stoudamire has the edge in his knowledge of the game, and smarts will always carry the day.

It's a challenge Stoudamire welcomes.

"The only time I get excited about playing teams I don't think are as good as us right now is when we play Philadelphia," he says. "The only reason I've got to go hard every time out against Philly is because I guess, from now on in my career, people are always going to be comparing me and Allen. The only way to settle that is to beat him — beat him often and beat him bad — and put up your numbers at the same time. There might be some nights when he has better numbers than me, but if our team wins, that's what counts." He laughs. "And I don't think there'll be *many* nights when he has better numbers than me."

If Stoudamire welcomes the individual challenge presented by Iverson, he welcomes more the chance to show his considerable talents against the best teams in the league. He's secure enough in his skills to be able to put aside his numbers for the team's good, if it's necessary. But until he's surrounded by better players, or until the other youngsters on the Raptors develop the same kind of all-round knowledge of the game Stoudamire's been building for nearly two decades, it will continue to be tough to win against the league's best.

The best players, of course, present Damon with his biggest challenge. Against the weaker teams, Stoudamire can pretty much do what he wants. It's more difficult for him to go up against teams that have depth of talent, who can put great defensive players on him and make every trip down the court difficult.

"Those teams will start overplaying me, not letting me get the pick or make the pass, and that's when it can get frustrating. I've got the ball, I'm seeing things, but I can't just blatantly point at a guy and tell him to go here or go there because that's all the defence is giving us.

"That's when you've got to have basketball smarts to see what the defence is doing, and you just have to let your basketball smarts or instincts take over. The trouble is, if you're not playing with four other guys who've got even a little bit of basketball smarts, you're going to be out there running around like a chicken with your head cut off. You might look stupid, but it's because someone else really doesn't know what's going on or what to do."

Darrell Walker, the head coach of the Raptors, fondly refers to Damon as a "player." Ever since he took over, Walker has spoken of his point guard's knowledge of the game and of the league.

"He knows how to play basketball, he knows the game. We've got some guys who just know how to play. I don't know if I can explain it better than that," said Walker. "If you know how to play, things are easier. If you're playing with other guys who know how to play, good things happen. Damon knows how to play the game. It's that simple."

And that complex.

There are times in games when Stoudamire must bite his tongue before his mounting frustration with teammates boils over into a confrontation nobody wants. From courtside, you can see him trying to direct someone to a certain spot on the floor with a quick flick of the neck, with a quick glance to the appropriate spot.

"We've got to get some people around him who think like him," says Isiah Thomas. "You could probably call him a student of the game. We have to get some other students around him."

That's a point with which Stoudamire thoroughly agrees.

The Raptors are a mishmash of backgrounds and abilities these days. They have to galvanize into a unit, which can be a time-consuming process. Doug Christie went to Pepperdine, hardly a college powerhouse. Walt Williams went to Maryland when Maryland was on the down side. Sharone Wright's years at Clemson certainly weren't littered with Final Four appearances. Carlos Rogers played at unheralded Tennessee State. Marcus Camby went to a Final Four with Massachusetts, and Oliver Miller played a bit part in an NBA final with the Phoenix Suns, but that's it. Each of those players knows the game and what it takes to become a champion on some level, but it'll be up to Stoudamire to bring them together and get them focused on performing consistently. The Chicago Bulls didn't become the best team in basketball overnight; there were lessons to be learned along the way, losses that toughened their minds and their resolve and eventually turned into victories. The Seattle Supersonics failed miserably before they reached an NBA championship series; Patrick Ewing and the New York Knicks, for all their individual greatness, have never won the big one.

Stoudamire will have to help carry the Raptors from the starting point to the ultimate destination. So far it's been hard, because in every game the team plays, Stoudamire might as well wear a target on his back. If the Bulls or Suns or Grizzlies or Sixers or Celtics or Pacers or anyone else can stop the point guard, it's unlikely the Raptors will win.

Each night, he takes a physical beating as well. Fans might see him buzz in and out of the key, see him drive to the basket and take on the big boys, but no one can appreciate what actually goes on unless they've done it themselves. Like Thomas has.

"The average guy in the NBA is like six-foot-six or six-foot-seven and something like 240 pounds, and when they put a hand on someone Damon's size or he runs into one of them on a pick, it's for real," says Thomas, himself just six-foot-one. "It's not some little touch. He has had to battle that ever since he picked up a ball — fighting the bigger, stronger guys — and for him to do the things he does takes about four times the effort of bigger guards. He does it every night, forty minutes a night, and I think people take it for granted. He has to be Mighty Mouse." (Stoudamire likes the comparison. "I want to be like him, sitting back and then flying in for the rescue," he says of the cartoon character whose likeness he has tattooed on his shoulder.)

To keep up that image takes a lot of dedication and hard work. After his rookie season, as he has in every off-season since he started playing basketball, Stoudamire went home and worked. He lifted weights, ran, worked on specific elements of his game. As one of the NBA's few left-handed players, he presents a different look to defenders because of his propensity to dribble with his left hand; that's something that's out of the ordinary. But being comfortable and being able to go to either side of the court opens up more options for an attacking guard, and he's just as adept with his right hand now as his left. It's a small part of his game but one that needed work, and he worked on it.

And then there are the weights and agility drills. Generously listed at 171 pounds in the Raptors' media guide, Stoudamire can drop down to the low 160s over the course of a long season playing forty of forty-eight minutes every game. He lifts weights during the season — most professional athletes do a modicum of weight-room work just to keep their conditioning up — but he works harder in the off-season. Thomas wasn't kidding when he spoke of the beating a player will take. Basketball might be a sport based on artistry — founder James Naismith had no idea it would develop into such a physical game when he first hung a peach basket on a wall at the YMCA in Springfield, Massachusetts, one winter to give his rugby team some way to stay in shape — but it is a war in the 1990s. Those are big bodies banging over a relatively small space.

"At the end of the first year, I was beat," says Stoudamire, who missed the last eleven games of that season with a combination of tendonitis in his knee and plain exhaustion. "I knew it was a grind, but I don't think I realized just how much a grind it was."

Driven to improve at every turn, Stoudamire arrived for his second season with a couple of new wrinkles to his game. He added a high-arcing layup shot, which gave him a chance against the seven-footers inside; he had a better move with his right hand; he was tougher defensively, where intelligence is as important as physical skill. Stronger because of the weight-lifting, he could physically steer players he was guarding the way he wanted them to go. It might not be apparent to the fans, but Stoudamire is strong, and he can move around much bigger players.

The game hasn't changed in the least from the one that Damon played back at Wilson High School, but the men he's playing against are bigger, tougher, and some are just as smart and driven. However, he's seen his own game improve from the time Dick Beachell sat him on the bench as a high school sophomore. He's worked to develop a style of play for twenty years. It has carried him from the playgrounds of Portland to the fame of the NBA, and he expects it will carry him to the pinnacle of the league in the not-too-distant future.

THAT ROOKIE SEASON

W HEN DAMON STOUDAMIRE arrived at the pre-
season training camp at Hamilton's Copps
Coliseum, he looked around and saw little to
get enthused about. Isiah Thomas, forced to pick from the
three unprotected players on each of the other teams in the
NBA expansion draft, had assembled a team short on talent
and long on long-shots. An expansion team is set up to fail
by the NBA, forced to dress a collection of misfits, castoffs
and players of dubious skill and dedication. Almost everybody on an expansion-team roster carries some sort of
baggage from his past. There are characters who have worn
out their welcome on other teams, and formerly solid players

whose skills have eroded substantially. The Raptors had a few serviceable NBA players, like Willie Anderson. Anderson played on some winning teams in San Antonio, but the quiet, smooth-shooting veteran was hobbled by legs so bad there were metal rods keeping them together. Tony Massenburg had a modicum of skill and Alvin Robertson, signed as a free agent after two years of retirement forced by a debilitating back injury, offered some hope. But Thomas's one-time teammate John Salley, a two-time NBA champion, turned out to be more comfortable being the team's unofficial recreation director and setting up parties than serving as a veteran centre providing leadership on the court. He was on the downside of his career, no doubt about it. And there were oddities, like 400-pound Thomas Hamilton, plucked from the Chicago playgrounds, and Vincenzo Esposito, a legendary shooter from the Italian professional leagues whose European style of play made him look as out of place as Hamilton. B.J. Tyler supplied the high comedy — he fell asleep after one workout with an ice bag on his leg, which caused so much nerve damage in the process that he never played in the NBA again. Tyler spent the 1995–96 season on the injured list before being bought out of the final four years of his contract by the Raptors.

"I thought, 'Oh, no. A bunch of screwups, a bunch of guys nobody wanted,'" Damon says. "We had like forty guys on the court, coaches and players, and I figured when we started to win, when we started to be something in the league, there'd probably be six of us left.

"It was going to be rough, but I figured I could lead them. There wasn't a lot of talent there, that's for sure."

Some of Isiah Thomas's veteran picks were able to help Stoudamire along. Alvin Robertson was a former NBA defensive player of the year who was as intense as any player in the league; he was nicknamed "The Raptor" by his teammates because he embodied the kind of intense attitude and on-court professionalism that Thomas wanted to instil. And Ed Pinckney was the voice of reason, a calming influence on the team's youngsters, most notably the rookie point guard.

"That first-year team was a lot of fun. I think, for me, I had more friends on that team. Don't get me wrong, I've got friends on this year's team, but that first team was an older team so a lot of the older guys sort of took me under their wing, so to speak. They showed me how this thing was run, how it was operated and how I could last longer."

He knew he had a lot to learn, and he was smart enough to go to the veterans for advice. Someday, soon perhaps, he'll be asked to provide that advice by some young player, and he wants to have learned from the pros what to say.

Even though the talent around him was dubious, and the lessons learned off the court about handling NBA life far more important than those learned on it, Stoudamire had great expectations for his rookie season. No expansion team in NBA history had qualified for the playoffs in its first season. In fact, of the four most recent franchises, Orlando, Charlotte, Minnesota and Miami, the Timberwolves' first-season record of 22–60 in 1989–90 was the best. Yet Damon dreamed grandiose dreams as he stepped on the court as an NBA player for the first time. He chuckles at the memory.

"When I came in, I came in thinking we could win right off the bat. We were going to shock the world and get to the play-offs the first year. I thought, 'I'm gonna take this team to the promised land.' I didn't tell anybody but I just had it in my mind. And then we started losing, and it sucked. No matter what I did, we weren't going to make it to the playoffs, and I was getting pissed off."

But losing is an expansion team's lot, even if Stoudamire wouldn't admit it right off the bat and would never, ever accept it. The NBA game is all about familiarity — knowing the strengths, weaknesses and idiosyncrasies of teammates, knowl-edge gained with the passage of time. It takes a point guard at least ten games to know just where a teammate likes the ball delivered, according to Stoudamire. For those reasons, the Raptors were destined to lose, and lose often.

November 4, 1995. The Toronto Raptors were about to play their second game in franchise history.

A night earlier, with 33,306 fans at the SkyDome providing an emotional lift, the Raptors enjoyed a storybook debut with a 94–79 victory over the lowly New Jersey Nets. For Damon Stoudamire, who finished with 10 points and 10 assists, that first game was unspectacular; his contribution was lost in the historic return of veteran off-guard Alvin Robertson. That night Robertson scored 30 points for the Raptors while adding 7 rebounds and 3 steals. Opening night was practically scripted: Commissioner David Stern was in the stands, the stadium was all gussied up, a Raptor victory was expected, and the home team didn't disappoint.

However, NBA reputations are made on the road, and against tough teams, and this night marked the start of a two-game stretch that was expected to put the young Raptors in their place, show them what the league is all about. Their first opponents away from the SkyDome were the Indiana Pacers and their next would be the Chicago Bulls.

The Indiana Pacers are the kind of team the Toronto Raptors hope to become someday, a deep team built around an all-star guard capable of challenging for the NBA championship. In the playoffs during the spring and summer of 1995, they came within a game of playing the finals, led by the sharp-shooting, trash-talking Reggie Miller, whose ability to get under his opponents' skin is legendary. Miller is the guy whose key basket finally silenced the heckling of rabid Knicks fan Spike Lee in his courtside seat at Madison Square Garden in the playoffs the year before. At home, playing against an expansion team, playing against guys who might not have the confidence to take his talk and dish it back, this should have been a cakewalk.

However, the news reports the next day told a different story:

The Indiana Pacers built a whopping 60–38 lead by half-time. It almost seemed the game was over, but in a marvellous and remarkable comeback, Damon Stoudamire led the Raptors in the second half as he poured in 26 points (7 of 23 field goals), including a perfect 12 for 12 from the foul line. Toronto clawed its way back into the game in the third quarter, outscoring the Pacers 33–13 and eventually taking a 4-point lead with just six minutes left in the fourth quarter. It seemed like the expansion Raptors were going to go two for two. But, in the end, the Pacers came back to beat Toronto 97–89 in front of a sellout crowd of 16,640.

Even though their second game in franchise history ended in defeat, one of 61 the team would suffer over the course of an adventurous season, it served to reaffirm in Damon's mind his place in the game.

"That was the game that told me I could hoop in this

league," he says. "I knew if I can do it against these guys, I can do it against anybody. The thing was, they got up on us by like 25 points, and we came back. I knew right then I could bring a team back almost by myself. I knew I could do it, and I knew everything would be all right."

Two nights later, the venue was Chicago's United Centre, the opponents the much-feared Bulls. The stakes were now considerably higher. The difference between the wretched New Jersey Nets and the dominant Chicago Bulls is night and day. This would be a very tough game, there was no doubt about that.

Unknown to anyone at the time was the fact that the big, robust, multifaceted Bulls were starting a march that would lead them to an incredible 72–10 regular-season record and, eventually, the NBA championship, thanks largely to Michael Jordan, the game's greatest player, who was starting his first complete regular season since his eighteen-month retirement and his aborted attempt to become a professional baseball player.

Jordan had looked mortal last spring in the Eastern conference semifinals, when the Bulls were beaten by Shaquille O'Neal and the Orlando Magic. Now, having had a summer to think about the ignominy of that defeat, and flanked by Scottie Pippen and Dennis Rodman, one of the greatest threesomes ever to wear the same uniform in the same season,

Jordan was out to prove a point.

The toughest competitor in the NBA, Jordan will take no insolence from some upstart rookie, and he will have no mercy on a franchise in its infancy. In fact, there is a history of bad blood between Jordan and Toronto general manager Isiah Thomas, a feud that goes back to Thomas's playing days, when his Bad Boy Detroit Pistons twice knocked Jordan and the Bulls out of the Eastern conference finals. Those were as much wars as basketball games, and now, with Thomas retired and the man most publicly associated with the Raptors, Jordan had every motivation to put on one of his usual punishing efforts.

No, this game was not expected to be pretty. Toronto, coming off the loss in Indiana two nights earlier, was expected to be little more than fodder for the machine-like Bulls. It might get ugly, and everyone knew it.

"Yeah, we knew they'd be waiting, but they want to beat everybody, not just us," recalls Damon. "We knew nobody was giving us a chance, but I don't think they realized that I could get something done against them."

Indeed he did.

The tiniest Raptor was at his best, beating Jordan off the dribble, beating him with pull-up jump shots, beating him up and down the floor. Jordan, generally considered one of the greatest defensive players in the game — a fact overlooked by his dominance at the other end of the court — was being eaten alive by a five-foot-ten lightning bug. It's not often number 23 fails to get the job done defensively.

"He lit me up," Jordan said after the game, a startling admission for the hottest star in the game to make about some no-name rookie on an expansion team.

Forget for a moment that Jordan scored 8 of Chicago's final 19 points and finished with 38 points as the Bulls battled back for a 117–108 victory. Stoudamire finished with 22 points on 8-of-15 shooting from the floor and 10 assists — his third straight double-double (double figures in two statistical categories). Even though the Raptors had lost, they had given the best team in the NBA all it could ask for. They had led by 8 at the half and made Jordan work as hard to a earn a victory over an expansion team as he would to earn a victory over any other team for the rest of the season. Stoudamire had left an indelible impression on the greatest player in the history of the game.

"Playing Indiana and Chicago right off the bat — damn, I was nervous. Indiana was one game away from the last championship, they were hot. Chicago — the only reason they lost in the semifinals the year before was because Michael Jordan was on vacation. Then, you're playing them early in the season, they've got their legs, nobody's hurt, they're fresh."

If there was any doubt about his place in the NBA, it was erased in the confidence-boosting performances against Indiana and Chicago. The rookie had gone on the road and put up two tremendous performances. His team didn't win, but he had shown enough strength that people started to realize more victories would come.

"I knew the league couldn't be like this all the time. I knew I had to hit some bumpy spots sooner or later, spots where you just don't play well. But those two games showed me I could do it. I could take over a game against the best teams."

Unfortunately, the euphoria of the opening-night victory, along with the promise shown in those narrow losses to Indiana and Chicago, quickly vanished. The Raptors' losses mounted. Stoudamire had a poor game, 8 points and only 2 assists, in a loss to Sacramento. Phoenix came to town and pulled one out in the dying minutes. The Raptors travelled to Charlotte and lost a heartbreaker in overtime. Utah won at the SkyDome with some excellent play down the stretch as the Raptors fell apart. Houston got a 3-point field goal from Robert Horry as the buzzer sounded to win 103–100 and handed the increasingly frustrated Raptors their seventh straight loss.

"It was getting really bad. We knew we weren't a regular expansion team — at least we thought we weren't a regular expansion team, because we had a lot of guys who had been in the league," Stoudamire says. "But we weren't winning, and everyone was getting pissed off."

Time to stop this, he thought. *Time to exert my will on the team, time to take command. Time to win.*

The perfect antidote for a losing team was arriving in Toronto wearing the uniforms of the Minnesota Timberwolves, the "anti-Bulls" of the NBA. The T-Wolves, one of the most recent expansion teams prior to Toronto and Vancouver joining the league, had travelled a slippery slope from mediocrity to despair in their seven seasons of existence. Poor drafting, bad management and under-capitalized owner-ship had made them one of the laughingstocks of the league. In fact, only the insistence of the league's head office kept the franchise from shifting to New Orleans. The arrival of former Boston Celtic and University of Minnesota superstar Kevin McHale as the vice-president of basketball operations, and the drafting of teenage phenom Kevin Garnett, had given rise to hope, but the T-Wolves were still considered one of the weak sisters of the NBA.

Some media observers in Toronto were calling the upcoming game a "must-win" situation for the Raptors, given the team's seven-game losing streak — a streak marked, as most of the season would be, by games lost in the fourth quarter when the opportunity to win presented itself.

"We play Indiana and Chicago and those types of teams,

those are the games I like playing because I know I'm the key, and if I have a good game, we're going to win. If we play middle-of-the-pack teams, those aren't my type of games because I can get lackadaisical sometimes. I know if I don't play a great game, we've still got a chance to win. I know sometimes I can get away with not playing well."

But, Damon thought, if the Raptors were going to the playoffs — hell, if the Raptors weren't going to be laughingstocks themselves — they'd have to beat the Minnesotas of the world. So he turned it up a notch, scoring a team-high 20 points while dishing out 13 assists and hauling in 7 rebounds in an easy 114–96 win.

The next night in Washington was another crowning moment — Stoudamire drilled a fifteen-foot jump shot as the buzzer sounded to give Toronto its first victory on the road. Winning on the road is a benchmark for any team, and for an expansion team, any victory away from home is a huge step in the right direction.

After the Raptors came home from Washington, Stoudamire had his best game by far against the Seattle SuperSonics, recording a triple double — the kind of statistical domination some players never achieve and a stat that separates the good from the great. He had 20 points, 11 assists and 12 rebounds on a game televised throughout the United States. But the wins were more important than the stats, for if

Stoudamire was to work his wonders as the leader of the young team, he had to show them how to win. It was also early in the season, and the playoff dream still fluttered in the back of his mind.

"Beating bad teams was always our problem," he says. "It's a problem we have to this day. I don't know why, it's just something about our team and our players."

It's also something he'll work hard to fix.

The highlight reel fast-forwards now to March 24, 1996, a Sunday in the SkyDome — a spine-tingling Sunday, as it turned out. The cavernous stadium is as ill suited a basketball arena as exists on this earth, with its thirty-storey-high ceiling and gradually sloped seating killing any feeling of intimacy. But even the SkyDome felt electric that day.

The crowd was almost unmanageable for an overworked staff. A Canadian basketball record and NBA season high 36,131 fans passed through the turnstiles to witness that afternoon's opponents — the amazing Chicago Bulls, who were by then well on their way to a 72-win season.

A home game against Chicago, with Jordan, Scottie Pippen and Dennis Rodman (in whatever hair colour he's sporting that day), is an event unlike any other in sport. The Bulls are like a travelling circus or a heavyweight prize fight.

Michael Jordan says that people come to see him play hoping he'll score 50 points and the home team will win. That pretty much sums up the mood of the thundering hordes who entered the SkyDome for an affair to remember.

In the Raptors' locker room, as coach Brendan Malone talked to the team, breaking down their opponents' strengths, his team's strengths and what would be the keys to success, Damon Stoudamire retreated into himself and his ritual pre-game concentration.

The Bulls knew he had skills that set him apart from any other point guard in the league, let alone any other rookie. In three previous games against Jordan and his merry band, Stoudamire had the 22-point, 10-assist game in Chicago in November; a 20-point, 13-assist gem when the Bulls beat the Raptors 113–104 at the United Centre three days before Christmas; and 26 points, 12 assists on January 18 at the SkyDome as the Bulls eked out a 92–89 win. Stoudamire knew Jordan and the Bulls would be gunning for him.

"There's something about the Bulls, they're the team everybody else wants to be like," Stoudamire says. "When you talk about the NBA, you talk about Michael and the Bulls. If we're ever gonna get to that level, where we win an NBA championship, that's the kind of team we'll have to be like. We use them to measure our progress."

And Stoudamire, pumped up by the drama of the occasion, found out he measured up quite well. He dished to his teammates, he dashed to the basket, he drained jump shots from everywhere but the seats as the packed stadium looked on in amazement and joy. When the historic afternoon finished, when Stoudamire looked up to the fans standing in the five-dollar seats hundreds and hundreds of yards away from where the action had taken place, the record book had been rewritten.

A career-high 30 points, 6 of 8 three-pointers, 11 assists and only 4 turnovers enabled the Raptors to beat the Bulls 109–108, a victory made even sweeter by the fact that Jordan hit an improbable jump shot from almost behind the basket that would have snatched victory from defeat had it not gone through a fraction of a second after the final buzzer sounded. Those six 3-point field goals gave Stoudamire a rookie-season record, eclipsing the 125 of Orlando's Dennis Scott, a mark set in 1990–91; and Stoudamire would finish the season with 133. He was like a giddy little kid when the game ended, leaping into the arms of his teammates, the conquering hero accepting the accolades of his followers. If there had ever been even the tiniest smidgen of doubt about his place in the game, that afternoon erased it.

"I give Stoudamire a lot of credit," said Jordan afterwards. "He has come in and played like a veteran."

For Stoudamire, who wants nothing less than to take the Raptors from their infancy to the NBA title, those words were sweet. But he refused to rest on those laurels.

"It's always great to beat the great teams," he said in the glow of the moment, as the fans hung around the SkyDome for nearly half an hour, cheering, or just standing and looking at the court where the improbable win had been played out. But the victory was tempered by Damon's drive for overall success.

"It's good for the fans, taking on Michael Jordan and all that, but we don't want to get too high after a win, too low after a loss. This was a great win, but we've got to start thinking about Atlanta and our next game."

One win is still just one win, and a victory in March might be good for the front office and the fans, but in Stoudamire's world, it was just okay.

"That might be the biggest win for the franchise to date, beating the best team, big crowd, all that shit, but it doesn't rank as my biggest win. It was a great moment, but by that time in the season we weren't going to the playoffs, that was for sure, so it was just a win."

Well before the end of his first year, it was obvious that Damon Stoudamire was far and away the best rookie in the league. Even in the early going, when he was still familiarizing himself with the league, its players and its demands, he realized that he had something special going. No other rookie was having as big an impact on his franchise; no other rookie was even being asked to do what he was being asked to do — take a group of misfits and mould them into some kind of cohesive unit.

Insiders around the NBA were taking notice as well. No other expansion team in recent history had started as well, and Toronto's marginally successful first month (4 wins in its first 10 games) brought reporters and television crews from across North America to the SkyDome and the team's practice facility, where they all wanted some time with the little prodigy. *Sports Illustrated* came by to do a piece, as did TNT, NBC's "Inside Stuff," writers from his home town, from Tucson where he went to college, and from major NBA centres across the United States. It was quickly apparent that he would be asked to play in the NBA's Rookie All-Star game in San Antonio in February. A couple of games earlier, Stoudamire had banged his shoulder, and he thought about passing up the opportunity to play. Then, the competitor in him took over.

The NBA's All-Star celebrations are like no other in professional sports. Always on the cutting edge of marketing its players, the league pioneered the weekend-long celebration now being mirrored by the NHL. The superstars of the day always carry the weekend — the Sunday evening All-Star game is regularly the highest-rated pro sports all-star game on TV — but the league is also mindful of the need to develop new stars to eventually take centre stage. So, a couple of years earlier, one portion of the Saturday night was changed from a Legends Game (an event that created little interest except among the macabre who wanted to see which old-timer would break down) to a contest among the league's top rookies, giving fans a chance to preview the young men who will turn into stars like Michael Jordan, Grant Hill and Shaquille O'Neal as their careers progress.

Playing with the best rookies in the league — including all six players chosen ahead of him in June's draft — Stoudamire treated the thirty-minute game as more than just meaningless exhibition staged for the league's corporate sponsors, who were more interested in the round-the-clock parties than the games themselves. He scored 19 points, dished out 11 assists and had 4 steals in just twenty-four minutes of playing time as the Eastern conference team beat the West 94–92.

"I really contemplated not playing," he said after accepting the MVP trophy and passing it over to his mom to take back to Portland, where it would be prominently displayed among the dozens and dozens of other baubles he has picked up over the years. "But then I started looking around San Antonio and the adrenaline started flowing. Isiah was calling my room, all these people were around and I wanted to play again. It was definitely worth it. It put the cap on a great first half of the season for me. I didn't feel I had to have a good game to prove anything or anything like that, but I wanted to have a good game for all the people who haven't seen the Toronto Raptors in person."

A couple of dozen rows up in the Alamodome stands, Isiah Thomas watched the game unfold like a proud papa. He had taken some heat for drafting the diminutive guard, had taken some heat for putting the growth of the franchise in the hands of a twenty-three-year-old. As commissioner David Stern handed Damon the most valuable player award, and as reporters and fans around the continent twigged to the talents of the expansion team point guard from way up there in Canada, Thomas stood, shook his fist in the air and smiled from ear to ear.

"People could see what we'd seen all year. People could see the unique skills he had, and instead of just hearing his name, they knew his game. I knew he didn't want to go, really. I knew he was tired. But I told him it would be good for him," said Thomas. "That was the closest he was going to get to the NBA finals for a while. It's good he got a taste of it."

But the thrill and excitement of the All-Star weekend would quickly fade as the regular season resumed. While Stoudamire had enjoyed his first fifty games, his first step onto the league-wide stage, even before he left San Antonio, storm clouds were setting over the franchise. Stoudamire, the rest of the Raptors and their increasingly large collection of fans were about to witness first-hand a bad case of growing pains.

The first head coach of the Raptors was the pugnacious Brendan Malone, whose appointment to the helm of the Toronto franchise was his first head coaching job since 1986, when he'd been a college coach at Rhode Island. He had gone on to be an assistant in the college ranks at Syracuse, Yale and Fordham before making it to the NBA, where he helped out on the bench with the New York Knicks for two seasons and the Detroit Pistons for seven — including championship seasons in 1988–89 and 1989–90, when Detroit won NBA titles thanks mainly to the play of superstar point guard Isiah Thomas.

Malone, purged along with the rest of the Pistons coaching staff early in 1995, first surfaced in Toronto during the team's inaugural free-agent camp in May, a weekend-long training session at Toronto's Seneca College for players who had been out of the league and were hoping for employment the next season. Trying to bring some semblance of order to a camp that included thirty or so players who were trying to at least earn an invitation to Toronto's first main training camp that October, Malone had handled himself well. The camp had run smoothly, giving Thomas and his scouting staff a chance to evaluate the players without having to worry that someone might be getting overlooked.

"We want someone who can tolerate the agony of losing while still teaching and getting across the message we want — that our only goal is an NBA championship," Thomas said after the mini-camp. "I think Brendan, who has been a great teacher in this league for many years, has the qualities we want."

Malone did appear, for public consumption at least, to be the type of teacher the Raptors so dearly needed. He knew the technical side of the game like no one else available to the Raptors. In nearly every game he could match up Raptors to opposing team players in a way that allowed Toronto to stay close to teams that had better personnel from number one to number 12 on the roster. But so much more is needed from today's NBA coaches. They have to balance a dozen different egos and handle the diverse personalities of players from varying backgrounds, with varying skills, greatly varying paycheques and even more greatly varying opinions of self-worth.

To Damon, that was one area of the job in which Malone didn't succeed.

"I don't want to talk bad about him, but I just didn't get along with him. I didn't like the way he handled people, the way he handled me. He wanted control all the time but he never listened enough.

"Having control — that's all fine and good, but I played for Lute Olson and he was just like Brendan. The first year I got there he was exactly like Brendan — really, really tight and hard to get to know. My second year, he loosened up a bit but he was still tight. My third year, he was just as loose as can be. My senior year, me and him were like this," he said, crossing his fingers in the universal sign for people on the same wavelength. "It could have been just like that with Brendan, but he never felt anyone out, he never gave anyone a chance, man. He didn't want to get to know us. Now that's not that important — he didn't need to know us off the court — but as a coach, you've got to understand your theories aren't right all of the time.

"You've got to listen to somebody. He didn't even listen to his assistants. Man, he just went out and did what he wanted to do."

Malone was a micro-manager during games, a trait that ran counter to everything that would allow Stoudamire — the franchise player — to excel. Damon likes to freewheel when he can on the court. A structured, half-court offence with a team like Malone had with the year-one Raptors did no good for either the point guard or his teammates. Malone used to ride Stoudamire about the number of shots the guard would take, ride him in private especially hard. Malone was astute enough to know not to criticize his players in public — especially the one entrusted with creating a winning franchise, the one so closely linked to the team's general manager, the man with the power to fire Malone.

"When you're playing with coaches who don't know their players, man, they don't know when they're on a roll. For all the superstars in the league — Jordan, Olajuwon, Barkley — when those guys get hot, do they call plays for the other guys? Hell, no. They say, 'clear out for that guy, he's going to work. He's killing his guy.'

"With Brendan, if I was killing a guy, it would be like, hey, we gotta slow down, we gotta set this thing up, call this play, call that play. The thing about it is, I don't think he blatantly disrespected me, or disrespected me in front of this team, but that might have been because he felt he couldn't win a power struggle.

"I think he knew how it was, but he didn't know enough about me as a player, what I could do for the team. If he came to me and was yelling at me and he had valid reasons, I wouldn't have any quarrel with him. The last thing I want is to get into a power struggle. I'm not gonna be the type of person who calls for a coach's head if he's not doing what I want to do."

But the private, unspoken criticisms — the glances from the bench, the insistence on spreading around the shooting and taking the ball out of the hot hand — irked Stoudamire no end. He couldn't understand why Malone would be irritated about the number of shots he took when anyone with even a passing knowledge of the game would realize the Raptors couldn't win if Stoudamire didn't score.

The brewing discontent came to a head during a west coast trip in late January, when the two got into a shouting match during a game. Stoudamire was angry. It was the only time Stoudamire publicly challenged his coach. "We were yelling and screaming at each other. I was saying, 'Hey, I don't shoot too much.' He was like, 'You ain't shit, we don't need you to shoot it.' It was bad, man. Real bad."

Stoudamire would have resolved his differences with Malone had Malone stayed around to coach longer than one year, because both men were going through a feeling-out period. They were getting used to each other, and they eventually would have found a way to co-exist. However, Malone was headed for a showdown with Thomas, a showdown he couldn't win. After all, Isiah Thomas was the man in charge.

It began with Thomas starting to publicly question some of Malone's decisions. The long season was taking its toll on Stoudamire, who played more minutes that season than any other rookie. Thomas wanted to look to the future, to see if the players behind Damon on the bench were going to be productive NBA players in the year to come. Malone, more concerned with immediate results, didn't agree. Players like

Jimmy King, Martin Lewis and Vincenzo Esposito languished on the bench night after night. Now, whether any of those players would ever have developed into regular NBA players is open for debate — King ended up kicking around the minor-league CBA in 1996–97, Esposito went back to the Italian pro leagues and Lewis started in the deep minors in Winnipeg before finishing the season buried on the Raptors bench — but Malone wasn't even thinking about the possibility.

"I know Brendan wanted to win games, and Isiah wanted to see young kids play and get through the season," says Stoudamire. "Personally, I hate losing and everything, but at a certain point, you aren't going anywhere like the playoffs or anything so you might as well let guys play a little bit who haven't been playing very much, to see what the hell they can do, whether they can play in this league."

King was the most glaring example of a young player not getting a chance to prove himself. One of the University of Michigan's much-vaunted "Fab Five," he was a second-round draft pick of the Raptors and was tabbed to fill a backcourt role behind Stoudamire and Alvin Robertson. King needed time in games to work on his shortcoming — he was only an average shooter and ball-handler — but he never got the opportunity. Because he played the same position as Stoudamire, Damon took notice.

"If Jimmy got a chance he might become a pretty good

combination guard, backing up both the point and shooting guard positions, because he's so athletic. Brendan never let him find out about that, never let Isiah find out about that," Damon says.

The festering private conflict between Malone and Thomas became an ugly public confrontation in the SkyDome on March 29 when Malone gave Stoudamire only twenty-nine minutes of playing time. As if to make a point to his general manager, who watched the game, seething, from his private location in an aisle off a corner of the court, Malone left a bunch of small, inexperienced players on the floor to absorb a 126–86 beating at the hands of the Orlando Magic.

"This isn't what we had in mind," a livid Thomas said at half-time of that game.

In another game, a week later, Malone left forward Dwayne Whitfield on the court for nearly an entire game. Everyone knew that Whitfield, the most mild-mannered six-foot-nine, 240-pound man on earth, had a bad knee, and everyone knew he would never be a major contributor to an NBA team. They also knew Whitfield, a rookie earning the league minimum with no contract past April, would never complain. Malone, again as if to test Thomas and make his point, left Whitfield on the court for forty-two of forty-eight minutes. Whitfield spent the next seven games in street clothes on the bench, nursing his chronically sore knee. Stoudamire, and a number of other people, lost a lot of respect for Malone that night.

"He ruined Whit in that game, just ruined him. Brendan kept him out there all night and everyone could see he was hurting. I don't know what he was doing. Why wouldn't he take Whit out of the game? Dwayne should have taken himself out. That's what he should have done."

That same day, Damon himself was put on the injured list, ostensibly because of tendonitis in his left knee, but in reality because Thomas didn't want Malone to ruin his prized possession. For public consumption, Stoudamire was hurt; in private, he was being protected. Thomas, the Raptors and everyone connected with the NBA knew that Toronto had a star in the making. Damon's career wasn't going to be threatened by getting caught in the middle of an argument between the coach and the general manager. Damon went home to Portland for about ten days while the team went on its last extended road trip of the season. He returned to Toronto to watch the last two home games of the season dressed in a suit and sitting at the end of the bench. The Raptors finished the season in last place.

The list of winners of the NBA's rookie of the year award is a chronicle of some of the greatest athletes ever to play the game. Bob Pettit won it in 1955, Wilt Chamberlain in 1960, the incomparable Oscar Robertson a year later. Willis Reed was a winner in 1964. Earl Monroe took it in 1968. The 1970s started with Kareem Abdul-Jabbar taking home the trophy, and the first award of the 1980s went to Larry Bird, who beat out a guy named Magic Johnson for the honour. Michael Jordan won it in 1985, Patrick Ewing a year later, and the 1990s began with Mitch Richmond winning. David Robinson and Shaquille O'Neal have their names inscribed on the trophy, as do Chris Webber and Grant Hill, who tied Jason Kidd for the honour in 1995.

So it was against this backdrop of greatness that Damon Stoudamire, his head freshly shaved thanks to an off-season whim, took to the podium in a SkyDome ballroom to accept his accolades in early May 1996. Isiah Thomas, as proud of this moment as of many in his own illustrious career, fairly glowed as he recounted the accomplishments of the franchise's first star.

"We knew Damon would be something special," beamed Thomas, "but I don't think any of us realized just how good he would be this quickly. People around the league are talking about him, people across Canada are talking about him, and we're just glad he's ours."

And with that, he planted a big kiss on his star pupil's cheek.

"Damon has given us a lot of joy and he's brought a lot to

this franchise, a lot to this city," Thomas went on. "He really put us on the map in terms of an expansion team, in terms of credibility and respectability. He really deserves this award."

The statistical story of Stoudamire's first season is startling. He averaged 19 points per game, 9.3 assists, 4 rebounds (an incredible stat, taking into consideration his size and the position he plays) along with 1.4 steals per game and 40.9 minutes of each 48-minute game. He started all 70 games he appeared in, missing 11 because of the late-season tendonitis and one because of a flu bug. His assist average was fifth-best in the entire NBA, first in the Eastern conference, and he ranked second only to New York's Anthony Mason in minutes played.

He led Toronto in scoring, assists and minutes played and came second in free-throw percentage, at 79.7 percent. He led all NBA rookies in assists, steals, free-throw percentage and minutes while finishing second to Philadelphia's Jerry Stackhouse in scoring. Twice, he was the league's rookie of the month, in November and in January, when he averaged an astonishing 20.4 points, 9.8 assists, 3.8 rebounds and 1.31 steals in 13 games — as good a stretch as any rookie has had in a long, long time.

"It's very meaningful for me that a lot of voters saw the importance of me to this team," he said that afternoon, grinning from ear to ear as he took the trophy from Thomas. "I think at the draft, a lot of fans didn't know much about me, and I guess that's understandable. I think I showed them what I can do, what kind of player I am."

Damon didn't take those fans who booed to task, even though he had the right to the biggest "I told you so" in years. He just basked in the accolades being thrown his way, as proud of his accomplishments as his effusive general manager was.

"It's great to watch him grow, as our franchise grows," Thomas said after the rookie of the year award was handed out. "I hope the people in Toronto and across Canada are watching because they are seeing something special."

The fans were definitely watching, and these days, they are cheering every move he makes.

THE SECOND SEASON

T HE SECOND SEASON IN RAPTOR history hadn't even
started. In fact, the full roster hadn't even been on the
court together. But by Labour Day 1996, Damon
Stoudamire was already setting a new standard of excellence for
his teammates — and himself — to attain.

The norm around the NBA is that players start filtering
back from their summer vacation about the first week of
September for some informal workouts with their teammates
in a sort of reacquaintance period. These workouts are relaxed
— just a bunch of guys playing ball, without a lot of structure
and little or no instruction from coaches. The idea is to get in
some running and some shooting and to start forming the

bonds that will develop among teammates over the long, gruelling season. It's an opportunity to joke around and reminisce before the formal, twice-a-day workouts of training camp, which begins in the first week of October.

Standing in the dwindling fall sunlight in a parking lot outside the team's Glendon College practice facility in the elegant Bayview-Lawrence section of Toronto, Stoudamire served notice that there were large goals to shoot for. In his quiet, determined manner, with no fanfare and just a recitation of what he saw as fact, he told some teammates that the Raptors were going to challenge for the playoffs, and that he was going to play in the league's annual All-Star game. Those were not goals to be taken lightly. Getting to the playoffs would mean practically doubling the number of first-year victories in year two. And for Stoudamire, making the All-Star team would mean absolutely no drop-off in his statistics, and no decline in his ability to carry his team. Yet by speaking those words and putting the goals on the table even before the first official workout, his stature as the team's leader was cemented. It said there would be no goofing around, and no excuses about being a second-year franchise with a bunch of new players and none of the experience of the rest of the league. It was a bold statement, but one Stoudamire knew he had to make to be sure everyone was on the same page.

"I don't want to finish last in our division. I don't want

to ever finish last anywhere again, that's for sure," said Stoudamire that day. "I don't think a lot of people took us seriously last year, and maybe we caught some people off guard in a couple of games. That's going to be different this year. We have to be ready right off the bat, we can't afford to start slow if we want to do what I want us to do."

Stoudamire had spent the summer months doing what he has done since he was a teenager — perfecting his game. After taking about a week off after the season ended, he was right back in the gym, working on specific areas of his game, areas he had seen room for improvement in during the grind of playing the world's best players night after night after night.

"I don't play a lot of five-on-five in the summer. I don't think you get better doing that," he says. "If you know just what you've got to work on, it's better to work on it alone or playing two-on-two or three-on-three. Full-court games are just playing, they're not working."

While other players coast through the off-season, hardly stepping into the gym all summer, Damon needs to stay in action, to continue his dedicated efforts to improve. The grind of an NBA season is taxing, and he has to stay in tiptop shape so he can began each season raring to go.

Isiah Thomas is no stranger to the work ethic needed for a small man to excel. "You walk around the NBA and go into those locker rooms and you see just how big those guys are and how quick they are. People are amazed by Damon's speed, but I don't think they realize just how hard he has had to work," says Thomas. "It's like David and Goliath, and this David has to stay on top of his game all the time.

"That's why the work he does in the off-season is as important as what he does during the year. He has to work hard just to stay on top of his game, and because he wants to be a champion, he's willing to do that. A lot of guys relax in the summer, they think they can take time off, but they can't. Damon realizes that, and that's what sets him apart. He's always striving to be better."

The Raptors who gathered for those informal workouts at Glendon College and began training camp in Barrie, Ontario, three weeks later were a very different group from the one that had ended the inaugural season. Coach Brendan Malone was gone, of course; he is now an assistant with the veteran New York Knicks, a job for which he is undoubtedly better suited. In his place, Isiah Thomas had hired Darrell Walker, an excitable, animated former player whose coaching experience was limited to just one season with Toronto as an assistant to Malone.

Gone, too, was centre Oliver Miller, who forsook the Raptors in search of a big-bucks free-agent contract before settling for the league minimum with the Dallas Mavericks. Alvin Robertson, Stoudamire's friend and confidant from that first season, was also gone, struggling through myriad legal and personal problems that would land him in a Texas jail, his comeback of a year earlier ended. Tracy Murray, the sharp-shooting forward who worked so well with Stoudamire in year one, had signed a huge free-agent deal with the Washington Bullets. The other veterans Stoudamire had become close to, Willie Anderson and Ed Pinckney, had been traded during the first season. Stoudamire now had to take their place, to be the sounding board for the kids, and even for some of the veterans who were back. At training camp, Damon would be named the team's captain, another logical step in his ascension.

"Yeah, I guess this is my team now," he said that day. "I have to take a bigger role, I guess, but everyone has to take care of themselves, too. Everyone has to be on the same page, but *they* have to do it."

Isiah Thomas knew that to keep Stoudamire's development moving forward — to be sure he wouldn't stagnate surrounded by players of questionable skills — he would have to attract a better group of players to camp. He spent the off-season reworking his team, picking NCAA player of the year Marcus Camby second in the college draft and sending Jimmy King off to Dallas in a deal that netted Toronto hard-working, low-maintenance veteran Popeye Jones, a workmanlike rebounder who knew his role and was more than willing to fill it. Thomas also induced free agent Walt Williams to sign a one-year, minimum-wage contract with Toronto, ostensibly to fill the shoes of Murray, but also in the hopes that he and Stoudamire would mesh and that Williams might eventually be talked into a long-term deal. Acie Earl, the gangly centre everyone on the team liked for his even temper, comical nature and ability to make everyone feel at ease, was back, the lone veteran to whom Stoudamire could go for advice.

As his second season started, Stoudamire knew he was a marked man. His rookie-of-the-year performance in 1995–96 set him apart from the rest of his rookie class and would for the rest of his career. He had to follow in the footsteps of the game's other young leaders — players like Grant Hill of the Detroit Pistons, Penny Hardaway of the Orlando Magic, Shaquille O'Neal of the Lakers and Alonzo Mourning and Tim Hardaway of the Miami Heat — if he wanted to elevate the Raptors to the league's upper echelon. Going into training camp he had a new attitude, one of expectation based on experience. He had spent much of his first year getting acclimated to the NBA; during the second he would have to become more vocal, on the court and in the locker room. It went with the territory, and it was a task he was willing to take on.

But if the pieces aren't there, the puzzle can't go together.

And while the 1996–97 season saw the Raptors continue their slow march to respectability, it was a march much too slow for someone with Stoudamire's impatience.

Sure there were high points, like Damon's triple-double of 21 points, 10 assists and 10 rebounds in a win over Shaquille O'Neal and the powerful Los Angeles Lakers at the SkyDome in the season's fourth game. But trying to acclimate Camby, Williams and Jones into the lineup took longer than expected, and upset wins of that proportion became few and far between. Toronto suffered through a six-game losing streak that began two games after that thrilling victory over the Lakers, and Stoudamire's dream for a quick start en route to a playoff berth was falling by the wayside. The games blended into one another: a win here, a couple of losses here; great games from teammates some nights, disappearing acts the next. Stoudamire's numbers were about the same as they'd been in his dazzling rookie year — he was averaging about 20 points and 9 assists a night — but the Raptors weren't piling up the kind of winning streaks they needed to get into contention. If not for the weakness of so many teams in the conference, they'd have been sliding into oblivion, and Stoudamire knew it. The frustrations were mounting, and he spoke night after night about the need for consistency.

As the dream of a playoff spot became increasingly elusive, Stoudamire began to focus on his other quest: a spot in the

NBA All-Star game. The league was celebrating its fiftieth anniversary in the 1996–97 season, and the All-Star break in Cleveland would be the highlight. The top fifty players in league history, including Raptors general manager Isiah Thomas and every player Stoudamire ever looked up to when he was growing up, would be there. For someone with a knowledge of the game as deep as his was, for someone who was as much a fan as a player, missing Cleveland would be a huge disappointment. He knew he couldn't expect to be voted to the starting five by the fans, but he did have a shot at being one of the substitutes added by the Eastern conference coaches.

The sting of the season's disappointing first half became even harsher on the night the substitutes were announced. Stoudamire wasn't among them.

"Nah, it doesn't hurt," he said at the time, the disappointment in his eyes betraying his words. "I guess winning counts for everything. We aren't winning enough, so I guess they think I shouldn't go."

If the Raptors weren't winning, they were certainly becoming more entertaining as the season wore on, and Stoudamire was having a ball. Coach Darrell Walker made a name for himself as a player with a helter-skelter, defensive style, and he wanted his team to mirror his personality. In a stark contrast to Brendan Malone's micro-management of the team in its first year, the blinders were off under Walker. He put his "Thin Towers" — the six-foot-eleven duo of Marcus Camby and Carlos Rogers — at the top of a full-court press and let Stoudamire scoot after the ball wherever it was inbounded. If the opponents scored, Stoudamire was under orders to get the ball back in and attack. It might have been physically wearing on someone not as well conditioned as Stoudamire, but all his off-season work and sweat were paying off.

There are no two coaches more dissimilar than Walker and Malone. Thomas came in for some criticism when he gave the man known as "D. Walk" the head coaching job, after Walker had spent just one season as an NBA assistant. Walker was an ex-teammate of Thomas's, a buddy, and many considered him just a puppet for the general manager. Walker has his foibles — he's not the best strategist in the game, and his animated nature sometimes gets in the way of rational thought — but he's a players' coach. The players trust him, and, for the most part, he trusts them. Damon was trusted from day one, and given the chance to run the team on the floor as he saw fit.

"Man, that Darrell," Stoudamire says, breaking into a smile and shaking his head. "Darrell got on my nerves sometimes, that's for sure. I'd be running up the court and I could hear him yelling my name and I'd be like, 'Ah, shut up man, let me go.' But I could go to Darrell during the games when he'd call some play and I could say, I don't think that's going to work, there's this or that going on on the court and we need to do this, not that.

"He'd say, 'Okay, you're out there, you can see it, I can't see everything from here. Go ahead and do it.' I would, and it usually worked. Even when it didn't, he'd never get all over me."

That he would even question his coach is a testament to Stoudamire's confidence as the team's captain. With Brendan Malone, he might have seethed, but he'd seethe privately. With Walker and his assistants — Brendan Suhr, John Shumate, Bob Zuffelato and Jim Thomas — he'd say what was on his mind because he felt comfortable doing it. Even with team-mates, during time-outs at crucial moments in games, he'd pull up a chair at the bench and tell everyone what was going to happen. Or venture out to the coaches and let them know what was really going on.

"You know how they'll go out there to their little huddle, well I'd go right out there and tell them, 'This isn't working, we gotta try this.'

"Sometimes I'd just sit down in the huddle and say 'To hell with all this, just give me that ball.' The point I'm making is we had that with D. Walk and the rest of the guys on the squad. I could give 'em that look and they'd say, 'Go ahead, take it over.'

"I remember that last game we played in Charlotte." It was the second-last game of the regular season, when there was little to play for and even less enthusiasm among many of the players. "We came in after playing in Milwaukee. I didn't shoot well against Milwaukee and I ended up missing my first five shots against Charlotte, but I kept taking them. In the second half, I hit my first jumper and I hear Darrell yell, 'Hey man, where's that been? I've been missing that for the last game and a half.'

"I'm like, 'It's here, I got it, just give me the ball. I'm hotter than anything. I ain't giving the ball up.' So that's okay, they'll let me do that sometimes."

Damon was proving to be more comfortable with his coach, and more comfortable with the players around him. With many of the veterans of the first year gone, it was up to him to assert himself as the team's leader. He was doing that, and enjoying it.

Damon didn't even bother to show up in Cleveland for the All-Star celebrations. Instead, he took his disappointment home to Portland and worked on a few things around his newly purchased house. After the break, he turned his attention to winning as many games as possible for his second-year franchise. The playoffs might have seemed like a pipe dream to most, but stranger things had happened, and if the Raptors could run off six or seven or eight wins in a row, who knew what the final outcome of the season might be?

What happened? The Raptors rattled off four losses in a row. The balloon was about to burst, and Stoudamire was about to explode. As the man in charge, he had to make sure everyone knew what was on the line. He had to speak up.

"I guess it comes naturally to me, but I think sometimes you've got to hold your tongue if you can't say a positive thing. Sometimes, I have to hold back because I don't know how to say negative things positively, if you know what I mean.

"You've got some sensitive egos on this team, and that's one big thing to worry about. In fact, that's one of the biggest things we've got to get rid of. We talked a lot about that near the end of the second year, how if we want to be a good team, people are going to have to put their egos aside and accept the roles they've been given."

And how does that happen? You win. It's amazing how some victories will change the mood of a team.

"If you're winning, that'll take care of a lot of things," Damon says. "Look at Philly. If Philadelphia had been winning a lot of games, then people wouldn't have been making a big deal about Allen getting 40 points a game at the end of the year," he says, alluding to Allen Iverson's scoring binge that resulted in four straight games of 40 or more points for him, but also resulted in four straight losses for the Sixers as the 1996–97 season drew to a close.

"If they were winning those games, then that would have been a major feat. But they weren't winning games. And then, it so happens, the game he doesn't score 40, he gets 11 assists or something and they win. People could say, 'Hey, you've got to pass a little more if we're going to win.'

"See, winning makes everything a little easier."

There will never be enough winning in an NBA season to satisfy Stoudamire until the season ends with him holding the Larry O'Brien Trophy, given to the league champions. That sets him apart from many players willing to accept less, and it's a lonely feeling. Stoudamire knows it, and it's something he finds difficult to discuss with teammates his own age.

"I spent a lot of time talking to Acie, when he was here. I talked to Doug Christie and I talked to Popeye and I talked to John Long and Earl Cureton, too," he says.

"But if you notice, the people I talk to are all older. If I went up to Marcus or I went up to Walt or Carlos or Sharone, I'm not sure they'd understand what I'm feeling."

One of the biggest challenges facing a team leader like Stoudamire is discovering precisely how to make those around him better, especially players his age. The veterans can take care of themselves. Stoudamire's legacy will be making the kids who are his contemporaries buy into the program. To do that, he has to be part athlete and part psychologist, and it's the latter that is always the most difficult. Because of his physical attributes, Stoudamire has no trouble making decisions on the floor that allow his teammates to flourish. He's the leading scorer on the team, the ball-handler, ball-distributor. He has an innate ability to get the ball to the shooter in the right position, and he can determine after just a few games who likes to get a pass about waist high, who likes it higher. He can learn if he should wait to make a pass until someone is in prime shooting posture; he can learn which teammate can take the ball on a bounce pass and work himself into shooting position. But knowing who needs a swift kick in the butt, who need some calming words, who can handle criticism and who needs constant reinforcement is a difficult task.

The reward for a right decision is seeing a previously average player perform above his level. But there are risks, too. It's not fun watching a borderline player lapse into self-pity and become a lost cause. Sharone Wright was Stoudamire's greatest test.

No NBA team can thrive without at least average play from their centre. Sharone Wright, for whom the Raptors traded away Ed Pinckney and Tony Massenburg in their first year, is the man on whom the team is banking to provide that presence. Trouble is, Wright is a sensitive young man, without the mean streak necessary to take the brutal pounding night after night against the game's best centres. Bothered by a bad back and wounded by the criticism of his play that became commonplace throughout the 1996–97 season, he was — and perhaps still is — on the verge of disappearing from the depth charts, of becoming just another case of unfulfilled potential.

Stoudamire, however, knows there is something worth salvaging. He's known Wright since they were teammates on the 1993 United States gold-medal team at the World University Games. He knows Wright wants to be better and has the potential to be an integral part of the Raptors' success. He just didn't know how to reach him. Until one night late in the season, when Stoudamire reached his breaking point in a game against the Miami Heat.

"I'm throwing the ball in to Sharone Wright, three passes I remember. Now, one of them was a bad pass, and I'm the first to admit a bad pass, so that one's my fault," recalls Stoudamire. "But I threw him two other passes, good passes and [Miami centre] Alonzo Mourning just threw him out of the way and took them from him. I said, 'I ain't ever throwing you the ball again if you don't start holding men off.' There's guys back in Portland I play with in the summer who know how to hold a guy off and get a pass.

"He yelled at me, I yelled back. He was like, 'C'mon man, give me the ball,' and I was saying no way. I was tired of it.

"Now, I've known Sharone for a long time, but I've never said anything like that to him before. I didn't want to sound negative because he took a lot of criticism during the year from everybody, and why did I want to give him more negativity? But that was the last straw. It was stuff that had been building up the whole year.

"Instead of sulking, though, and just getting and staying mad at me, he got 14 points and had a good game from then on. He was probably pissed at me but I couldn't care. I told him, 'If that's what it takes, I'm going to cuss you out every game.' I guess that's what I have to do."

That moment took Stoudamire's relationship with a friend on the team to a new level and helped reinforce the importance of his role as the team captain. He can't be everybody's buddy; he's got to get in a few faces, lay down the law and let everyone know what's expected.

"It'll be interesting to see what happens," Stoudamire says. "Sharone had a back problem, he got out of shape, but I think he'll come back in tiptop shape and ready to play. He's so tired of people picking on him — me, the coaches, the media — I think he'll come back in tiptop shape, for sure. Then, it's just waiting to see if that comes through on the court every night."

Stoudamire knows now, however, that he can do something to help make Wright be better. He knows, too, that he can probably do that with every player on the team. No one but his teammates saw the little confrontation with Wright, and that's the way Stoudamire prefers it most of the time. However, he also knows there is a time to let his frustration out in public to send a message, one he has delivered loud and clear a few times.

In an anteroom off the hallway outside the Raptors' locker room, reporters wait after every game to get the wit and wisdom of coach Darrell Walker. These mini news conferences follow a cooling-off period of about ten minutes, and they are designed to give the beat reporters a chance to get the coach's insights before they invade the locker room for the bon mots of the athletes themselves. On the evening of March 3, they got more than they bargained for.

The Raptors had just returned from a seven-game road trip feeling pretty good about themselves. They had won three of the seven and would have won four if not for a particularly wretched last-second foul called on Doug Christie that allowed Indiana's Reggie Miller to make three free throws in the final seconds of the game. The playoffs were still miles away, but things were going well. Until the evening of March 3, that is, and the team's appalling loss to the Boston Celtics in a game that marked the low point of the entire season.

The Celtics were among the worst teams in the NBA in the 1996–97 season, bearing no resemblance to the storied franchise that had won more NBA titles than any before. There were no Bob Cousys on this team, no Larry Birds, no John Havliceks, no Bill Russells. A clownish sort of character, M.L. Carr, coached the team, a man as far removed from Red Auerbach as one can imagine. This was the kind of team the Raptors should have beaten handily, especially at a time when they had been playing so consistently well.

That's why that afternoon's 107–103 loss was particularly galling, bad enough for Walker to warn the media to "be gentle" in the post-game scrum.

As the writers milled about outside the locker room, an obviously miserable Stoudamire stormed out. There was no doubting his anger as he tore off down the hallway, his sudden, sullen departure catching the media so much by surprise that no one had time to even think about asking him a question. Not that it would have been answered. His stormy departure was the first public display of a private anguish that had been building inside Damon for most of the season.

The next day, he put it in perspective.

"I'm a winner. I've been winning games my whole life, and to lose games is frustrating. If you're not frustrated, you shouldn't be out on the court."

What ticked him off the most, he said, was having his team laughed at by the laughable Celtics, who had won just 11 of 54 games coming into that game. Being mocked by such a bad team was the last straw, and, in private, Stoudamire let his teammates know how he felt.

"It's good to see him act that way sometimes," said Walker. "It showed he cares and it showed he's not going to accept losing. We need more of that around here."

It was hard for Damon to accept that some of his teammates might not be as concerned about the signal that one game was sending as he was. Everyone knew how he felt; he had to be sure others felt the same way.

"We've all got to care. Basketball is five people, it's not tennis. I'm not the only one out there."

And then came the words of warning, words that he had been storing up inside him for some time:

"We don't have an identity as a team," he said. "Until we start winning games that we're supposed to win, we're not going to have an identity. Right now, we just have a cast of characters. We have nothing significant going on. We're trying to get to that point but we're caught in a flux — we're not just sorry, but we're not good. We're in the middle, standing there.

This team could go either way."

He was bound and determined not to let it go the wrong way.

There was a moment late in that second season, however, when Stoudamire saw everything fall into place as if he had scripted it. It was a game against the Detroit Pistons, and any game against the Pistons has a special significance for the Raptors, who desperately want to beat the team that Isiah Thomas spent so much time with. However, whether it was because they tried too hard to prove something to their general manager, or whether it was just because the Raptors did not have the firepower to stick with the talented Pistons and their superstar, Grant Hill, Toronto had lost the first seven regular-season games they played against Detroit. On March 19, though, something clicked.

"The game I was most impressed with for the whole season was when we beat Detroit in Detroit," Stoudamire recalls. "That night we played that game as if we were a team going to the playoffs. We had beaten Philadelphia the night before in Toronto, and I was tired in Detroit, knocked right out."

Good teams know the way to beat the Raptors is to stop Stoudamire, and they all try to make the littlest Raptor work hard for everything he gets.

"They were picking me up full-court all night. I just had no legs. I had to work every time I touched the ball.

"I didn't have anything to give them that game except that, by being on the court and being a threat, the other team doesn't know if I'm tired or not, so they've still got to respect me. But that night everybody came up big. Doug hit a big 3-pointer late in the game, Marcus had a monster night, and it turned out to be the best game of the season to me. I had 11 points and 2 assists, but we won.

"That's when I knew we were eventually going to be okay. That's how good teams win games — when everybody contributes, when somebody like me might not have a big game but the team still finds a way to win. That was the biggest win of the year because it showed everybody that we could do it even if I just had a bad night."

After that win in Detroit, the season played itself out: the Raptors never got too hot for too long, but they never got too cold. There were moments of greatness and moments of mediocrity that blended into each other. Now the playoff dream was nothing more than a distant memory, and Walker and Stoudamire set their sights on achieving a 30-win regular season, which would represent a nine-game improvement from the previous year and a solid foundation on which to build for the future. The Raptors went into the final two weeks of the season almost at their goal, and Stoudamire had to convince his teammates it was worth working for.

"What you've got to do is sell your teammates on the fact that you've got to win some games down the stretch, you've got to finish strong to come back next year with a positive outlook. We have to come out and play strong against teams to give them something to think about for next year," he said. "If you don't come out and play hard every night it can get ugly, and it was getting ugly for us.

"Two games in a row, we had blowouts, to Orlando and Washington, and those nights, it was like some guys would go into the games and not care if we won or lost, like it didn't make any difference to them."

The Washington loss was particularly ugly. The Raptors gave up more than 40 points in the first quarter alone and never had a chance to get close. They played as though they didn't care, and not caring is the worst sin imaginable to Stoudamire.

"I remember we got beat up in Washington bad. They beat us really bad from start to finish, and it was embarrassing. It gets really embarrassing when teams are jumping all over you, beating your ass, and everybody's laughing and giggling at you. I said, 'Hold on, something's wrong here, something's really wrong.'

"I didn't know how the hell we were going to get those thirty wins, I didn't know how we were going to do it, but we were going to start whipping some people and we were going to start smartening up. I wasn't taking any of that Washington shit any more. I said there were too many games left and if they wanted to screw around, they could do it without me."

He could have taken the rest of the season off, perhaps gone on the injured list with some fabricated reason. It wouldn't have been the first time a star took a little break as the season wound down. But that's not the kind of player Damon wants to be. He wants to get out there and compete, whether it's for his team's thirtieth win in a sour season or the NBA championship. He told his teammates in no uncertain terms that he expected them to shape up.

"I guess it got through because we got our thirty wins and ended the season on a two-game winning streak."

As the curtain fell on the 1996–97 season, the Toronto Raptors were much better off than they had been a year earlier. Stoudamire was more secure in his leadership role, one the team so desperately needed him to fill. In Marcus Camby, there was a solid front-court complement to Stoudamire's backcourt wizardry. In Doug Christie, there was a guard to take some of the pressure off Stoudamire, lessen his offensive load and handle the difficult defensive assignments. Zan Tabak was an oft-injured but at times solid centre. Martin Lewis was a bit player, but he brought a great amount of athleticism to the team. Sharone Wright is expected to increase his productivity in the coming season, and Carlos Rogers might develop into a solid role player who brings particular skills to the team.

But it remains up to Stoudamire to make sure everyone blends, to make sure the personalities and physical skills mesh. He knows it's going to be hard, but with two seasons in the NBA under his belt, he is much more adept at gently massaging the egos and personalities of his teammates and drawing the best out of all of them. He'll be watching to see how their minds work as much as how their arms and legs operate. He knows he'll be called on to massage a few egos on the long road to the top of the heap.

"Right now, we've got minor egos, and I think some guys' egos are being stroked by outside influences because I don't think anyone on our team is a bad guy by himself. I think we've got a lot of people on our team who are easily persuaded, to the point where someone from the outside, someone not connected with the team, can come up and say, 'Hey, man you're supposed to be playing, what the hell are you doing not playing over this guy?'

"And some guys think, 'Yeah man, he's right, I should be playing over that guy. Look what I do when I get in the game.

SITTING ONE OUT: A solitary figure taking a break from a practice, Damon sits in front of an empty section of SkyDome stands. Come game time, those stands are full and the people are there to see Stoudamire perform.

Richard Lautens/Toronto Star

DOUBLE TROUBLE: Rod Strickland and Chris Webber of the Washington Bullets (now the Washington Wizards) present Damon with one of his usual problems every game — the double team. *Ken Faught/Toronto Star*

TALKING IT OVER:

Damon and head coach Darrell Walker often discuss strategy, with Damon able to suggest plays or situations in a game the team should exploit. Walker, a former player, takes some of those suggestions to heart.

NBA Photos/Ron Ng

THANKS, DAMON:

It's safe to say Isiah Thomas was pretty happy when his team's point guard was named the NBA's rookie of the year in 1996. Thomas capped off the awards presentation by planting a big kiss on his prize player's cheek.

NBA Photos/Ron Turenne

MAKING THE PLAY:

Aside from being a prolific scorer, Damon can always find an open teammate for a pass. Here, he gets one off in heavy traffic during a game against the Boston Celtics. *NBA Photo*

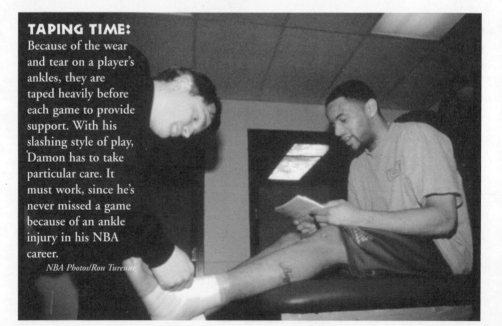

TAPING TIME:

Because of the wear and tear on a player's ankles, they are taped heavily before each game to provide support. With his slashing style of play, Damon has to take particular care. It must work, since he's never missed a game because of an ankle injury in his NBA career.

NBA Photos/Ron Turenne

SIR CHARLES AND I: Charles Barkley doesn't have much good to say about too many teams in the NBA, but the outspoken Houston veteran says he thinks the Raptors are on the right track.

Michael Stuparyk/Toronto Star

NOW, WATCH ME:
Putting on clinics for would-be Raptors is part and parcel of the job. Here, Damon shows his stuff to a group of youngsters during one of the many public appearances he puts on each season.

Andrew Stawicki/Toronto Star

ICING DOWN:
Ice is the cure-all for the average NBA player. The pounding a player takes over the course of an 82-game season makes him extra careful to take all the right precautions.

Tony Bock/Toronto Star

UP IN THE AIR: On defence, Damon can disrupt teams in a variety of ways. He can make steals against other point guards or get in the passing lanes to stop teams trying to score.

Steve Russell/Toronto Star

GUARDING THE GREATEST: "He lit me up," Michael Jordan said after the first meeting with Damon Stoudamire. The Raptors beat the Bulls once in each of their first two seasons.

Tony Bock/Toronto Star

A STOUDAMIRE SANDWICH: It gets tough sometimes when you're the man with the ball. Stoudamire finds himself in difficult situations time and time again, as he did here in a Celtic double-team.

Jeff Goode/Toronto Star

CLEAR THE TRACK: Damon tries to work his way around the imposing presence of Patrick Ewing of the New York Knicks. The Raptors and Knicks wore throwback uniforms to 50 years ago when the then-Toronto Huskies and New York Knickerbockers played the first game in NBA history.

Ken Faught/Toronto Star

MAKING A STATEMENT: It didn't take long for this huge wall mural to adorn a building near the Toronto's SkyDome. Damon's immediate impact on the city was measured by the fact this took the place of one depicting the dramatic home run by Joe Carter which won the 1993 World Series for the Blue Jays.

NBA Photos/Ron Turenne

FAITH 10"

COURAGE 8'11"

DESIRE 7'1"

DAMON STOUDAMIRE HEIGHT 5'10"

I do this, I do that. I'm better than such and such a player.'

"What we've got to make sure is that people understand their roles and understand what they have to do. And that's something you've got to deal with from within yourself. Everybody's not going to average 20 points a game in this league, everybody's not going to be an all-star, and everybody's not going to get a big, fat contract.

"But the bottom line is, when it's all said and done and you did what you had to do and what you're capable of doing, everyone's going to live comfortably, everyone's going to have a big house, and everyone's going to have a big car.

"If you've got inner peace, you're never going to have a problem, but if you don't have inner peace, you're always going to have a problem, especially if you're trying to get somewhere you can't go or be something you're not.

"That's the only thing I can see tearing this team apart, and I've got to try to find a way to make sure it doesn't happen.

"I don't think it's ever a bad thing to want to play more, because if you quit wanting to do that, you should quit playing the game. But it's another thing to understand what your strengths are and what your weaknesses are and what you bring to the team. If you can accept that and if you can understand that, then everything will be fine.

"That's what we've got to get across to all our players."

6

ISIAH AND DAMON

THE ENTERTAINING AND CONFUSING saga of the Toronto Raptors' ownership began in 1993. That year, three different groups petitioned the NBA for the right to own the league's first international expansion team. The league, in fact, had no plans to expand and only agreed to consider the applications when the Toronto groups forced the issue by submitting non-refundable $100,000 (U.S.) application deposits.

Of the three, the winner was a group headed by Toronto catering magnate John Bitove, Jr., who had enlisted the aid of the Bank of Nova Scotia, broadcaster Allan Slaight, former Ontario premier David Peterson and long-time Bitove family friend Phil Granovsky in his bid.

Bitove, who graduated from Indiana University when Isiah Thomas was playing college basketball there, hired Thomas as the team's first general manager and also offered his long-time idol a 9 percent ownership stake when Thomas joined the franchise.

That arrangement didn't even last until the team's second season, however. In November 1996, Slaight exercised a clause in his ownership agreement that forced Bitove to buy his share or be bought out himself. When Bitove was unable to meet the obligation and was forced out, Slaight ended up with a majority share, 79 percent, with 10 percent owned by the bank, 9 by Thomas and 1 each by Peterson and Granovsky. Slaight went on to obtain the two smallest shares, giving him 81 percent as the second season ended.

Slaight, however, said almost immediately that he wanted to divest some, if not all, of his shares. And in Isiah Thomas, he found a more than willing purchaser. Thomas is as accomplished a businessman as he was a basketball player. He's the owner of the largest quick-copying business in Michigan, with several other top-flight business interests that have have provided him with an inside knowledge of the machinations of the world of high finance. He envisioned turning the Raptors into a total entertainment entity, something along the lines of the Disney Corporation, with, of course, the basketball team as the centrepiece of the business.

But as the night of Monday, April 21, 1997, arrived, negotiations between Slaight and Thomas's ownership group, which should have been relatively simple and easy to consummate, were bogged down and in danger of falling apart completely.

The Bank of Nova Scotia, with its 10 percent, had the right of first refusal on any sale and, quite understandably, it didn't want Thomas and his banking partners to take control and edge it out of a lucrative business proposition. It had been in on the ground floor, and it wanted to reap the benefits of the franchise's growth.

Thomas had let it be known that he was willing to resign as general manager and vice-president and walk away from the franchise if he and Slaight couldn't reach agreement on the sale by that Monday night, one day after the end of the regular season.

As that deadline day wore on, Thomas was stymied, more frustrated than angry, he said. And that was having an effect on the players. When the general manager made it known that he was willing to walk away from Toronto, walk away from his investment, walk away from all the brilliant moves he had pulled off on the basketball side of the operation, Stoudamire knew that he, too, must walk.

"Isiah Thomas means so much to me and so much to my

teammates," he told the media. "I appreciate everything the people have done for me, I appreciate what the organization has done for me, but I can't see myself playing here if Isiah's not with the team. When I came out of college, no one wanted to pick me as high as he did, no one believed in me like he did. He put his faith in me and we made each other look good."

It was a startling show of loyalty in what is generally perceived as an era when money talks in professional sports and loyalty lasts only until a better contract offer comes along. "Isiah means so much to me, I don't want to be here if he's not. I think it would be best if the Raptors trade me and get something for me because when my contract expires after my third year, I won't re-sign here."

There was no doubt Stoudamire was speaking from his heart, and no doubt there would be takers. New rookie salary rules, agreed to by the NBA and its players' association in 1995, had imposed a restricted pay scale and a three-year limit on rookies' contracts. Under those rules, Stoudamire had a deal that paid him more than $7 million for three years, but he would be an unrestricted free agent following the 1998–99 season, able to strike a deal with any team willing to make him an offer. Given his skills, leadership abilities and age, teams would be lining up to get him, and everyone connected with the Raptors knew it.

That's why Stoudamire's nerves were a little on edge as afternoon turned into evening that Monday, and he waited at his home for word on what was transpiring, word that was slow in coming. If the deal fell apart, Thomas would be gone, perhaps as soon as the next morning. Toronto had finished a successful 30–52 regular season the afternoon before in Boston, and Thomas, in his annual year-end address to the team, had made it sound as though the talks were progressing as he wanted. But Stoudamire knew the world of high-stakes finance was tricky, and the slightest wrong move could scuttle Thomas's deal. He wanted to stay — he had a definite affinity for Toronto, the Raptors organization and its fans — but he didn't want to stay alone.

"I have a great relationship with Isiah, I don't have any relationship with Mr. Slaight," he had said that afternoon, after the players had gone through their end-of-the-year physicals before heading to their off-season homes and vacations.

That's what made the night so pivotal to the franchise's history. If Thomas walked — and he was absolutely prepared to — and then Stoudamire walked, all the good that had occurred in the first two years of the Raptors' existence would have been undone. Who would Slaight be able to entice to become general manager, and replace a man who had taken on guru status with many of the players and fans? All the promise of two seasons under Thomas's guidance hung in the balance as the phone calls and faxes flew back and forth that night.

Word finally filtered out about nine o'clock that Thomas and his partnership had signed a letter of intent with Slaight to purchase a majority share in the team. A quickly convened news conference in the boardroom of the team's downtown office building was called to lay the plan out. Thomas had won, and the sighs of relief around the office were audible. If there had been a microphone in the general vicinity of the team's franchise player, another sigh would have been heard as well.

"That's great, great news," Stoudamire said later that night. "Now everything's gonna work out for the best. Isiah's staying, and I'm staying, too."

The 1980–81 Detroit Pistons were one of the NBA's worst teams. Finishing the season with a 21–61 record — exactly the same mark as the first-year Toronto Raptors — made them the second-worst club in the twenty-four-team league, behind only the absolutely wretched 15–67 expansion Dallas Mavericks. The Pistons had been led by John Long, who averaged 17.7 points a game, and Kent Benson, Phil Hubbards and Keith Herron played key roles. It was a long, long season of small crowds, consistent losses and growing frustration.

But the draft in the summer of 1981 netted the single most

important pick in Detroit Pistons history, the selection of point guard Isiah Thomas, a six-foot-one sophomore who had left the University of Indiana early under what was then known as the NBA's hardship exemption. Given the poverty from which he had come in Chicago, it wasn't difficult for him to prove the need for the money that would come his way. The day general manager Jack McCloskey announced the selection of Isiah Lord Thomas III as Detroit's first pick, second overall behind Mark Aguirre, was the day the Pistons franchise turned around.

Thomas quickly displayed the skills that McCloskey knew would set him apart from the rest of the league. In his first season, the Pistons improved to 39–43, missing the playoffs by just four games as Thomas averaged 17 points and 7.8 assists a game. In 1982–83, the 37–45 Pistons again missed the play-offs, but Thomas continued to improve, increasing his scoring average to 22.9, his assists to 7.9. In 1983–84, Detroit made its move. Thomas led the team in scoring at 21.3 points per game, and the 49–33 Pistons made the playoffs, narrowly losing in overtime to the New York Knicks in the fifth and deciding game. They were on their way to the top, and Isiah Thomas was taking them there.

Their progress continued over the next few seasons. First came a trip to the conference semifinals in 1984–85, a series that ended with a heartbreaking loss to the Boston Celtics;

then another playoff appearance in 1985–86, this one ending with a double-overtime loss to the Atlanta Hawks in the first round. In 1986–87 they had a breakthrough year, with 52 wins in the regular season and easy playoff wins over Washington and Atlanta before a brutal, seven-game conference final against Larry Bird and the Boston Celtics, a series the Celts would win, with a score of 117–114 in the deciding game. But it was during the following season that Thomas, who had become the unquestioned leader of the NBA's best up-and-coming team, truly made his mark. With 54 wins, the Pistons won the Central Division title, while Thomas averaged 19.5 points per game. They knocked off Washington in the first playoff round, dumped Chicago in the second and finally got past their arch-rivals from Boston in the Eastern conference championship. The NBA final was a classic affair that the Los Angeles Lakers won in seven games despite some record-breaking heroics from Thomas, whose performance in game six of that series was as exciting as any before or since. He scored an NBA record 25 points in a quarter, made an NBA record 11 field goals in the fourth quarter of that game and made an NBA record 14 field goals in the second half — this despite the fact that he had severely sprained an ankle in the game's dying minutes. That the Lakers won game six by a score of 103–102 did little to diminish the now-legendary performance. And even though Los Angeles would win game seven,

108–105, and with it the NBA title, Thomas cemented his reputation as a winner, and someone who could carry his team on his back. He averaged 21.9 points, 8.7 assists and 4.7 rebounds in 23 games — superstar numbers by anyone's estimation.

The next year was the culmination of everything Thomas had been building towards from the time he left Chicago for Indiana. The Bad Boys were crowned NBA champions after a 15–2 run through the playoffs ended with a sweep of the Lakers in a four-game final. Thomas averaged 18.2 points, 8.3 assists in each playoff game and the vision of him clutching the ball after the final whistle, tears welling in his eyes, told you all you had to know about his feelings about being called a champion.

"As great a player as he was, what he did best his entire career was lead," said Chuck Daly, who coached the Pistons through their championship years. He was speaking in early 1996 at a ceremony to retire Thomas's number 11 at the Palace of Auburn Hills — the sparkling arena in Detroit's northern suburbs affectionately known to many as "The House That Isiah Built."

Detroit would repeat as world champions in 1989–90, and Thomas would shine once again. He was the most valuable player of the playoffs, averaging 20.5 points a game as the Pistons went 15–5 in the post-season and knocked off the

Portland Trail Blazers, in a relatively easy five-game final series.

The journey from rookie on a bad, bad team to the height of basketball supremacy took Thomas eight years and more pain, suffering and dedication that many can imagine. He asked no favours and gave none in his rise to the top. His single-minded determination to win set him apart from those around him and allowed him to elevate his game and the game of his teammates. Now, as he stands each night in an aisle off to a corner of the SkyDome court, watching Stoudamire weave his magic, he must think and hope he's watching an image of himself starting on that journey to the top. He knows the sacrifices he had to make, and he knows his point guard can make them, too.

"If you want to win a championship, you have to have a singular type of focus," he says. "There are only two things that exist in your life — basketball and your family — and the rest of the world sort of doesn't exist, it kind of falls by the wayside. You become so engrossed with basketball, during the season, during the summer, that it almost becomes an obsession. You're not interested in any other conversation, don't watch anything else on television unless it's basketball. If you could go back and talk to Bird, to Magic, to Jordan, to myself, we all had it, and I think Damon has that, too."

But it comes at a cost. While universally respected for his abilities on the court and for his passionate desire to succeed,

Thomas wasn't in the game to make friends. When he was trying to assess Stoudamire's psychological make-up before he drafted him, before he anointed him with the title of franchise-builder, he was trying to find out if the young man had that kind of personality, that kind of drive. The answer was obvious.

"Look at him, he's five-foot-ten. If he was weak-minded, he'd be dead. Of course he has it. You talk about all the other guards who are coming into the league, [Philadelphia's Allen] Iverson, [Minnesota's Stephon] Marbury, Stoudamire, [Phoenix's Jason] Kidd, and the only one they're ever linking to a championship is him.

"He wants a championship, and that's already set him on a different path, a path you have to travel down alone a lot of the time because you're chasing something totally different. Iverson and Marbury and Kidd and all of them might put up great numbers, but I don't think anybody's making a connection in their minds between them and a championship like they are with Damon, who you can just tell by watching wants to win every time he steps on the court.

"Those guys will all be great players and have great careers, but he's the one who's going to take his team to a championship. Having that kind of responsibility, taking a team all the way, scares the shit out of a lot of people because you're going against the grain, against people's ideas that a good career and a good contract are all they need. Ninety-five percent of the players in the league, if they get a championship or not, they don't care. Damon is willing to make the sacrifice to travel that path.

"I started on that path when I was about seventeen and I'm still on it, I guess, just in a different role. But I tell him, the gratification and the rewards are worth the effort. It's a very small club, that championship club. A lot of people want to get in but a lot don't want to pay the price. Damon does.

"We're trying to convince the people of Toronto that we're not about just making the playoffs or trying to have a nice thing going where people come and pay their money and it's nice. From day one, we've said we want to win a championship, we want to be in that club, and we want Damon to take us there.

"I think he's willing to go into the dark cave for seven, eight, nine, ten years, trying to find that ring, that championship up there in the darkness and finally come out with it and say, 'See, I got it.'"

Is he?

"Yeah, of course," Damon answers almost before the question's been asked. "Winning is the only thing. There's nothing like it, nothing. Second place ain't worth nothing, second place is for losers. Nobody remembers who came in second. Losing, to me, is the end of the world. I know we're losing now and I hate it, but it's going to make winning all that more sweet."

Thomas is in the process of doing his part to surround his court leader with players who can complement his style. In off-guard Doug Christie, he's found a dynamic defender with the kind of slashing offensive game that plays perfectly off Stoudamire. Finally given the chance to play substantial minutes, after being obtained from the New York Knicks in one of Thomas's shrewdest trades, Christie has blossomed into an excellent all-round player. "I think Doug and I are one of the best young backcourts in the NBA, and people are really going to see that," Stoudamire says.

Aside from Christie in the backcourt, Stoudamire can look to the team's front line with some optimism, because it is there that Thomas has added young, inexperienced Marcus Camby, who followed Stoudamire in 1996 as the team's second first-round draft pick.

He's long — six-foot-eleven with arms that seem to go forever; lean — 220 pounds on a still-growing body that found it hard to take the routine pounding of an NBA season; and youthful — twenty-three years old. Camby can give Stouda-mire something every point guard wants — a big man who will take the ball and score. In his rookie season, Camby showed flashes of brilliance, and took some of the pressure off Stoudamire, but those flashes were too few and far between. "I don't think Marcus knows how good he can be," coach Darrell

Walker often laments. "If we can just get him to stay healthy and get some consistency in his game . . ." His voice trails off.

Stoudamire would also be amazed by his young buddy at one moment and somewhere near exasperation the next. "Marcus has to realize what the NBA's all about, realize what kind of work is needed all the time. He's got great skills. He can do a lot of stuff out on the court, and we just have to make sure he can do it consistently all the time."

But Stoudamire is the key to the future, as he and Thomas well know.

"There's always room for improvement in my game," he says. "Getting stronger, maybe finding a few new moves. You never stop learning how to play in the NBA. I've had a couple of seasons against these guys, and I know how they play and what they like to do and what they don't like to do. I know what our squad needs to do to get to the next level, and I think everybody else does too."

The pay-me-now-or-I'm-gone philosophy of many professional athletes these days turns off the fans. Most fans want some continuity in their team. They want to develop a relationship with their players; they want to see the same faces night in and night out. It bothers the media, too, who see on a daily basis just how money drives the game in this age of multi-million-dollar contracts. Purists can't quite grasp the peripheral lure of "cross-marketing opportunities" which bring a whole new dynamic to the sports situation, a dynamic that has nothing whatsoever to do with how a player defends a pick and roll, how he handles himself down the stretch of tight games, how he elevates those around him to play better when something is on the line. Sports, these days, is not about sports at all; it's about money, it seems.

Loyalty, however, goes both ways. Players who bolt from one team to another lured by a much more lucrative contract are often portrayed in the public as villains, ingrates who follow the green instead of the dream of championship. When Shaquille O'Neal left the Orlando Magic for a seven-year, $120-million contract from the Los Angeles Lakers, he was chastised from coast to coast. "He's just chasing the movie deals, the rap album deals, the shoe deals," people said. "It's a slap in the face to the franchise that gave him his start, helped him get famous," they say — a franchise he took to the NBA finals in 1994, a franchise he finally blew off in the blink of an eye for money so big it's incomprehensible. But teams, general managers and owners have to show some loyalty as well. They have to nurture their players, make them feel secure in their roles, make sure they understand those roles. There are ways to foster goodwill and to make players feel wanted without opening the vaults. In fact, under the NBA's stringent salary cap rules, managers have to be creative. Making a statement with a paycheque is not an option, at least not to rookies, whose earning potential is capped.

Thomas's relationship with his players left them all feeling wanted and appreciated, even if their paycheques weren't as large as they would have liked. The afternoon media session with the players before that Monday evening negotiating deadline was filled with platitudes for the general manager; there wasn't a single player who didn't express his gratitude and affinity for Thomas. They would all have looked elsewhere for employment as soon as they were contractually able had the Thomas-Slaight negotiations broken off.

It is hard to explain satisfactorily the hold he has. It's referred to in some corners as "The Cult of Isiah."

"It's easy, he's been through everything we're going through," Stoudamire says when asked. "When he talks about something, he's not just talking about what he thinks, he's talking about what he knows."

If nothing else, Thomas knows he can relate to his players on a level that makes them feel comfortable. Hell, he can put on the sneakers and shorts and T-shirt and go one-on-one with his best player, as he did in a memorable best-of-three series with Stoudamire after one of the team's practices, a little session in mentor versus student that Stoudamire barely won as the rest of the team and a handful of writers and broadcast reporters looked on in amazement.

A survivor from the gang-infested streets of the west side of Chicago, Thomas broke into the NBA with as much in the way of street smarts as anyone in the league. But he didn't have the smile of Magic Johnson, the country charm of Larry Bird or the acrobatic style of Michael Jordan, the three players with whom Thomas is most often linked. He was, to more than one observer, a cut-throat competitor to whom victory was the only acceptable end. Winning was what drove him, not magazine covers or feature stories, and certainly not the opinions of magazine or newspaper writers or television talking heads.

"I don't want to do endorsements, I want to own the company people are endorsing," he's been widely quoted as saying during his playing days, summing up a philosophy that has created a self-made multi-millionaire. That's the winners' mentality for which he is universally known, the give-no-quarter-ask-none philosophy he's instilling in his Raptors.

"We don't come to play, we come to win." That was the Pistons' motto, and Thomas has adopted that same philosophy with Toronto. His ultimate goal is an NBA championship for the Raptors, and it is that kind of determination that has been Thomas's calling card at every stage of his career. With the Pistons, he led his team to the 1989 and 1990 NBA titles. The team was revered in Detroit, reviled elsewhere. Bill Laimbeer, the Bad Boy enforcer on a team known for its rough-and-tumble style of play, is one of Thomas's biggest supporters. And yet Thomas once punched Laimbeer in the head in a particularly nasty practice dustup — he hit him so hard that he actually broke a bone in his hand.

If Thomas was far from Mr. Nice Guy when he played, that didn't matter. He was a winner. He made a lot of money for his teammates and he became a champion, and that's what sets people apart. Sure, he's going to the Hall of Fame. As a matter of fact, his Detroit coach, Chuck Daly, once said that if Thomas were five or six inches taller he might have been the best player ever to play the game. But others have speculated that his single-minded approach to winning might have cost him some of the peripheral accolades and endorsement opportunities that lesser players have enjoyed. Thomas, however, isn't bothered by those missed opportunities. He's secure in his place in the game as a champion.

Thomas did finally learn to play the league's off-court game, of course, by osmosis, by maturing, by coming to realize how the NBA really worked — but he never lost the edge that set him apart and made him the winner he will forever be known as.

It's that kind of political awareness and hunger for championships that makes him a perfect mentor for Damon Stoudamire.

Sure, they can play one-on-one, and Thomas can show

Damon how to get off a jumper with a defenders' hand in his face, he can tell him and show him how to grab hold of an opponents' jersey away from the referee's glance, he can demonstrate how to lock down an opponent by leaning on his hip while defending him and steering him whichever way you want him to go. But Thomas can also tell his protégé how to play the all-important political game. It's that kind of knowledge of both sides of the NBA game that will prove invaluable to Stoudamire as his career goes on and he gets closer to the dream of an NBA championship.

"It didn't hit me until I was twenty-six or twenty-seven years old, the politics of being in the NBA," says Thomas. "I had to get burned a few times before I learned how things worked and what I'm trying to do with him is not let him get burned. I can tell him my experiences — he doesn't have to step into that fire and get burned too. He can avoid that sort of thing and get to the point he deserves to be at with a little less trouble than there was for me.

"It's things like what players have to do to be respected in the league, how important the media's job is as it pertains to a certain player," he says. "I learned, and I'm trying to tell and teach Damon, it's not how good you play entirely, it's really what the media says about you. If they don't say you can play, guess what? You can't. That's basically the game. Magic understood, Bird understood, Jordan understood. I was like him, I think. I was alone when I came into the league, I didn't have the marketing machine and all that stuff behind me. I came in and it was like, 'Hey, I'm lacing them up, I'm ready to play, I'm gonna go out and tear everybody up.' I didn't know there was this whole other part of the game. I can tell him there is, and maybe accelerate the learning curve for him."

An all-too-familiar scene plays out in the Raptors locker room, deep in the bowels of the SkyDome. As the media pour into the smallish room — the franchise has precious few permanent facilities and must share its accommodations with visiting rock bands, baseball teams and football teams — they invariably head to a corner just off the walkway that leads to the court. It's there they find Stoudamire, the unofficial spokesman for the rest of the players, the man from whom everyone wants an assessment of his play, an assessment of his team's play and an assessment of that night's opposition.

It's not a role Stoudamire relishes, but it's one he knows he must perform, simply because he's the best player on the team, the one most recognizable to the fans. All too often he's explaining why his team didn't win, why something fell apart at the most crucial moment of the game. Often, it's because someone missed a shot, made a wrong move, forgot to cover the right man on defence.

Stoudamire is developing a good rapport with most of the Toronto media, few of whom question his skills, desire or leadership abilities. There has been some sniping — he shoots too much, he can be surly after defeats, he doesn't suffer silly questions very well — but none of it bothers the young guard. He's learning how to open up, how to trust, how to accept the criticism that is part and parcel of fame.

"The only thing I don't like is when they try to get you to say stuff because they know it's going to look good in the papers or on TV. We can't talk about the referees, but they try to get us to talk about them all the time. And we're not going to criticize our teammates, or talk negative about them. I think the Canadian media's a bit different than the States. Down there, they want to tear you down instead of building you up. Up here, they don't go looking to make trouble for everyone."

At the other end of the locker room most nights, Isiah Thomas stands watching the scene unfold. He is a man who has had more than his fair share of negative things written and said about him, a man who understands that he's fair game for comments based in fact or fiction. Thomas is able to shrug off most criticism because it comes with the territory (you get the adulation of some fans, you suffer the pettiness of others), but on the court no one can question your skills. He's trying to show Damon that the final score and the statistics measure one's worth in the eyes of those who really matter — your teammates.

Most nights in the Raptors locker room, it could just as well be Thomas in that corner, as a young Detroit Piston upon whom the future is resting, answering the same questions about the same kind of losses more than a decade earlier. *Been there, done that, don't want to see it again.*

"That's why I can feel for him on those nights," says Thomas. "I've got to get people around him who think and feel the way he does about the game, the way it should be played and what's important — winning. I need to get people in here he can influence and bring into that little cave I was talking about.

"Does he have that ability to influence right now? I'm not sure, but I know he's got it inside him, and it's just a matter of growing and maturing and letting it come out. Hell, he's five-foot-ten and he intimidates the shit out of people. They don't feel absolutely threatened but they know there's something different about him, something that sets him apart, and I think it's that focus on the ultimate goal. Whereas there are some guys who are seven feet tall who you can approach quite easily, he's not exactly like that. He has that presence you hear about, and it's something you've either got or you don't. When you walk into a room, you can tell. Damon's got it, people know it, and he just has to learn how to use it with the players on the team. It's just a matter of him learning how to use it and us teaching him how to use it."

There is some deference shown to Stoudamire by his teammates, and it comes from his special place in the franchise's pecking order. It's not because of some teacher's pet kind of situation, where everyone knows Stoudamire has the ear of the general manager who signs the cheques and hires the players; it's not because he's the highest-paid player, because under his first contract he wasn't. It's because he's the best player on a young team and he's the guy around whom the future will be built. Talk to any Raptor and they get the idea. Or, if they don't, they get led out of town.

Damon understands that role and has grown comfortable with it.

"Yeah, I am the leader, and I don't mind," he says. "I don't think I lead necessarily by saying a lot of stuff or talking to individual guys a lot, but I lead by what I do on the floor. I think everyone sees how much I want to win, and I want them to have the same ideas and goals. That's why they got me here, that's what my job is, so that's what I do — lead by example."

But Stoudamire knows there is a price to pay for leadership, just as there is a price for fame. Leaders, especially those on sports teams, live in a bubble, detached from the teammates they are trying to lead. By the very nature of the relationships — "C'mon, watch me, trust me, follow me" — there has to be some distance. Stoudamire doesn't have a lot of close friends on the team — friends, sure; close friends, not really — and that leaves him few places to turn. So he turns to his general manager.

"Isiah's a great help, he's sort of a sounding board," says Stoudamire. "I can bounce things off him, maybe get some advice, and that really helps me. I guess he's just got a perspective that helps me out. I don't use the relationship against anyone, I won't bad-mouth my teammates to him, but there are things he's done that have helped me out."

The ties that bind Isiah Thomas and Damon Stoudamire run much deeper than basketball and their place in the game. The astounding influence of two strong mothers, and their careful adherence to the right path, have as much to do with their bond as anything else.

Isiah Thomas grew up in poverty on the west side of Chicago, where drugs and danger lurked at every turn. It was a society that claimed many young men who did not have the strength to resist the pull of the gangs. Mary Thomas, to whom Isiah speaks nearly every day, was the pillar of strength in the family, and she helped create the savvy businessman and future Basketball Hall of Famer who now runs his own franchise.

To hear Isiah Thomas talk about his mother, left to raise him and his family by herself when his father left, is to hear a story of love. He likes to tell how Mary Thomas invited rival gang leaders into her home in an effort to sponsor at least a temporary truce in the battles that raged on the streets where her sons had to grow up. He likes to tell the story of his family having to switch apartments repeatedly when they couldn't pay the rent; he likes to tell the story of having to go to school with his older brothers long before he should have enrolled, so his mom would know he was safe from the streets and the gangs and drugs and the chance to make wrong decisions for which he would pay for the rest of his life.

He likes to tell the story of his mother's strength, how she sacrificed so he and his brothers would have every chance to escape their circumstances.

So, too, does Stoudamire like to tell tales about his mother: how she made do with less for herself so there were always presents on Christmas morning, how she would use her income tax refunds to send him to basketball camp, how she kept him on the straight and narrow.

While the circumstances were slightly different — Stoudamire's neighbourhood was much less dangerous in the 1980s than Thomas's was in the 1970s — the similarities are clear. Thomas and Stoudamire both knew they were going to be professional basketball players when they were in high school, and playing the game at the highest level is what drives them.

"That's your joy, that's your security," says Thomas. "Being in front of 25,000 fans and having the pressure on you and all that, that's when you're most comfortable and that's where you have no problems. You don't have to think about your brother or your sister or your mother or your dad. All you have to think about is putting the ball in the basket."

Thomas was able to grow from a raw rookie into a respected veteran who felt the ultimate joy of victory, a feeling like no other for a professional athlete. He now is charged with guiding the development of Damon Stoudamire from raw rookie into a respected veteran and champion. It should be a joyful process to watch.

7

LIFE IN THE LEAGUE

AFTER THE CHEERS FADE and the fans leave and the arenas grow dark, NBA players turn quickly from heroes into humans. The tug of ordinary day-to-day life is something their fans can easily relate to — maybe the kids are sick, or an argument is lingering with a spouse or a girl-friend. Maybe somebody in the family is trying to get through some personal crisis, and it's weighing on the player's mind. Maybe it comes down to the question of just what to do next — go home, go to a club, get something to eat somewhere.

For Damon Stoudamire, there is little glamour once the lights fade. A week of two-a-day workouts at training camp, eight pre-season games hither and yon as the NBA and its teams spread the word to outposts from one coast to the other, an eighty-two-game schedule dotted by long road trips divided by one-night stands and late-night flights culminating in, hopefully, a six-week run in the playoffs — all of this amounts to much more grind than glamour. One of the biggest adjustments he's had to make in moving from the structured regimen of college athletics to the free-flowing life of an NBA star is how to handle the abundance of idle time. Practices at home, at least under coach Darrell Walker, begin at mid-morning and seldom last more than a couple of hours. Even with pre-game strategy sessions and warm-up drills and post-game interviews, game nights at the SkyDome seldom involve more than a five-hour commitment. In the locker room, there's always a ball boy to fetch a fresh towel, an attendant to pick up the dirty ones, take the uniforms to be washed, lay out the gear for tomorrow's practice or game. Travel is all first-class — no more than twenty-five people generally, on a chartered jet — so the biggest responsibility a player has, with the Raptors at least, is getting himself from the downtown SkyDome to the airline hangar.

From there, it truly is a pampered life. Someone takes your bags and drops them at your hotel room in the next city while someone else brings the bus onto the tarmac and delivers you to your hotel door. A bus picks you up the next morning for shoot-around, brings you back, picks you up later that day for the game and hauls you off to the door of the plane later that night. It's the sort of pampering that makes life easier but it also makes it pretty monotonous. It can get old in a hurry.

"I like to shop — electronics stuff, clothes, maybe a nice pair of slacks or a shirt," Damon says. "On a road trip, where we go to more than one city, I might hit the stores for a while, kill some time, see what I can pick up. There's not a lot of excitement to fill the days."

It can be downright boring, in fact.

"You've got to be able to handle the loneliness," says Isiah Thomas. "You've got to like yourself. And you've got to like hotel rooms. A lot."

It didn't take Stoudamire long to figure that out.

"My rookie year, I was probably like every rookie in the league. I went out a lot at the beginning. I was trying to go to every club that people had always been telling me about in the different cities," he recalls. "But by about the sixth game of the season, I was so tired, I thought, 'I can't do this for my whole career, I've got to change up.'

"From that time on, I learned how to live in the hotel rooms. After you play ball, you just go to the room and learn to live between those walls and be content and watch a lot of Spectravision."

At home, Stoudamire's main method of escape is the same

as it's always been — basketball. After home games, or on off days when the team is still in Toronto, he generally retires to his lakefront condo, which is sparsely but tastefully furnished and decorated, and does what a lot of young, bored men do — he turns on the TV and gets settled on the couch, all the while working a little on his professional development. It's homework without the books.

"I watch a lot of basketball," he says. With his little satellite dish he can get anywhere up to ten games a night on his big-screen TV. "That's what I like to do. I don't watch games like a lot of other people watch them, though. I like to see how teams match up against each other, who's guarding who, what guys do to break down certain other guys. I look for the games within the games."

With thousands of dollars of disposable income (and with a lot of restaurants, bars and clubs willing to pick up the tab just to have an NBA player in the house to attract a crowd), a lot of players — especially the young, single ones — like to hit those night spots. Maybe they'll dance a little, listen to the music, maybe meet a young woman, or maybe just hang with a couple of teammates or other close friends. Some like to throw private parties in clubs, and Damon likes to make the rounds every now and then. (A New Year's Eve fête ex-Raptor John Salley hosted once ended with a car in Lake Ontario.) Damon and Penny Hardaway of the Orlando Magic co-hosted a little get-together when the Magic had a night off in Toronto one time, but Stoudamire's appearances at such events are the exception rather than the rule.

"I try not to hang out during the week. I might occasionally pop up in a place here or there for a little while, but never for too long. I don't really go out to eat that much. If I do go out in public, I generally get something to go. I think a lot of restaurants in Toronto are probably mad at me," he laughs, "because they probably don't even serve to go, but they kind of deal with me."

If the schedule has the Raptors playing on a Saturday night at home and off on the next day, Stoudamire will step out for a little while just to unwind. But if a club doesn't hold any allure, he might just hang around his apartment with someone like teammate Walt Williams, who lives in the same building, or Marcus Camby, who lives in an apartment building down the street.

Sometimes it's just a pain to go out, not worth the aggravation every recognizable celebrity must put up with. Autograph-seekers are everywhere — in the restaurant between the appetizer and main courses, in the clubs between songs, in the streets. "I can't believe it sometimes," says Damon's mom, Liz Washington, who makes a couple of trips a year from her Portland home to Toronto to visit her son. "He'll come around from the SkyDome parking lot to pick me up at the hotel, and people are just there staring at him. One time, we were driving away and this lady had a video camera and she was taping him just driving. I said, 'Damon, does this happen all the time?' I mean, we weren't doing anything, just driving, and they wanted to get it on tape. That must take some getting used to."

"Yeah, it does," he admits. "But it was like that in college, and I understand it's going to be even more in the NBA. I don't have to like it a lot but I have to realize it's going to happen and there's not a lot I can do about it.

"Probably the one thing every NBA player hates is when they go out in public and somebody gets to talking about basketball," he continues. "That's the last thing on your mind. You just want to get away from it, but people want to keep bringing it up. When I'm out, I like to keep a low profile most of the time."

Low profile or not, if Stoudamire is out, he's going to look good. Despite the trappings of his position and the people he could hire to take care of his every whim, he's not about to let anyone near his wardrobe.

"I don't trust anybody with my clothes, I like to wash them all," says the man nicknamed "Felix" during his college years for his resemblance to the "Odd Couple" neat freak. "I remember one time I had somebody wash my clothes for me and they shrunk my shirts, they really messed them up. If I do it, I know I'm going to get it right."

There probably has been no more dramatic moment in Toronto sports history than the home run Joe Carter of the Blue Jays hit off Philadelphia's Mitch Williams in the bottom of the ninth inning of game six at the SkyDome to win the 1993 World Series. It sent the city into paroxysms of joy and made Carter a hero to even the most casual baseball fan. It also sent the marketing wheels spinning at companies that wanted to capitalize on their association with the slugger and his historic blast. A couple of long fly balls from where that homer landed in the left-field bleachers of the SkyDome, a painting of Carter's memorable shot was quickly emblazoned on the side of a building, a larger-than-life tableau created by one of the companies Carter had done endorsements for. People figured the painting would last forever as a testament to the moment. But "forever" didn't last too long. Soon after the little point guard on the newest team in town started taking the city by storm in his rookie season, the Carter tribute was painted over, replaced by a picture of Stoudamire driving to the basket. Paid for and produced by one of the companies Stoudamire was working for, it demonstrated that the Raptor rookie had arrived as a marketing force.

"I was amazed because of the significance of what that Joe

Carter picture stood for. That was history, and for them to replace it after several years with me was something special."

Because Stoudamire became synonymous with the Raptors, the player around whom the franchise would be built, his attraction to businesses blossomed almost as quickly as his game. People were quick to jump on his bandwagon, lining up to be associated with a young man who could bring their company name to the minds and wallets of the adoring public, or at least the adoring kids who could convince their parents to spend some money. He was becoming a superstar, and everyone wants endorsements from superstars.

These days, the money to be made outside of the game is often more substantial than an athlete's salary. Having a celebrity or star athlete as a spokesman can create millions of dollars in revenue for companies. Michael Jordan picks up about $30 million a year from companies that want his name associated with theirs. Stoudamire, as the first true basketball star in Canada, can't command that kind of money from Canadian companies but he can make inroads into virgin territory. If he wants.

"If I played in the States, I think I could probably be doing a lot more than I do in Canada," he says. "I sometimes don't think Canadian business people at this time really understand the market and what NBA players mean to the people. That's something they're going to learn, though, and it's something I have to deal with and accept for now.

"I think right now and in my first couple of years, they might have been a little scared, not knowing whether I was going to be in Toronto, but it'll help with a long-term deal because that shows I'm going to be around for a while. It'll help, too, once they realize how big basketball is going to become, and I think they'll start trying to do more things."

Indeed, his American profile is at least as big as his Canadian one. And simply because of the size of the market, bigger, better and more offers pour in. In his home town of Portland, one of the most popular sporting goods stores in the city has a life-size cardboard cutout of Stoudamire prominently displayed. In a store in Florida, it's the same thing. The national television advertisements he does are all over the screen. He gets calls and offers from everything from shoe companies to car companies to clothing companies and every kind of company in between. Damon has mixed emotions right now about taking advantage of everything on this side of his career.

"At first I didn't really like doing any of it, but I guess it comes with the territory, and I became a lot more comfortable with it between my rookie year and my second season. Sometimes it's boring but now I understand it's part of the business, and it's going to help me out in the long run because I won't be playing ball forever."

Because of his stature, he's able to pick and choose, and he's careful to avoid over-exposure. "People come to me with deals but I don't think it's wise that you take every little thing that comes your way. For instance, I have a deal with Kellogg's, and to me, Kellogg's is right up there as one of the top products in the world, and that's the kind of company I want to be associated with."

"Crossover marketing" is a buzzword these days — think of Michael Jordan in the movie *Space Jam* or Shaquille O'Neal as a Grammy Award nominee and movie star. Damon has spent part of each off-season the last couple of years in Los Angeles, checking out the television industry and seeing if that's something he might like to do when his basketball career is over. That is, if he can handle the pace. An athlete used to going full speed every second he is at work, Stoudamire finds the pace of television, well, not so quick.

"What I find is that actors have a unique talent and I can certainly appreciate the stuff they go through and I can appreciate how hard it is to do what they do," he said after a stopover in Los Angeles shortly after his second season ended. "It's a nice job but you have to put up with a lot of stuff. You've got to sit in a room for maybe three or four hours until they call you down to the set. You've got a lot of idle time, and to me it was boring. I had fun, but it was boring at the same time. I don't think I could do it all the time. Maybe a little bit but not all the time."

Unlike scores of other players who practically turn their lives over to agents, friends, family and the omnipresent sycophants who see a quick way to make a buck with every basket and victory, Stoudamire has decided to chart his own course. He has allowed his father, Willie, to become his business agent and his best friend, Erin Cowan, to be Willie's assistant, but they are really assistants, people who take care of the nuts and bolts. The decisions are made by the man himself. He's seen teammates and friends sign with agents with high profiles and many of the game's greats as clients, but he's also seen those teammates and friends practically ignored. He figures if someone represents a Michael Jordan and some borderline player, that borderline player will never get the attention he needs to increase his visibility and marketing potential. Stoudamire's certainly more Jordanesque than borderline but he won't let anyone make decisions for him.

"I've just got to have control over what's going on in my life," he says. "It just hit me one day that I didn't and it really pissed me off. I was sitting at home and I thought, 'I'm tired of having to call this person or that person to get this done, to do that. I'm a grown man and I shouldn't have to do that.'

"This probably will sound petty to some people, but if I lose my pager, why the hell can't I just call the pager people and tell them instead of calling someone else because that other person knows who to call and they think they have to do everything for me. It's little stuff like that. I'm too smart for that. I know what I want to do with my life, I don't need people for little stuff like that. I need people to oversee some things and help handle a lot of the day-to-day business but I don't need people to make decisions for me."

If there is a criticism of Damon, it is that he seldom lets his guard down. But when you think of where he's come from, it's easy to understand why he won't let too many people get too close, why he seeks relief from the bright lights by withdrawing into his private world.

"No, I don't trust a lot of people," says Stoudamire. "I think I'm smart enough to realize that people just want to get close to you so they can get something for themselves.

"Anyway, I take things people say with a grain of salt. Sometimes I'm listening, sometimes I'm not when people are talking to me. People just say stuff because they think it's what you want to hear. I'm a person who's always trying to better himself, on and off the court, and I don't need people just hanging around trying to be my friend by telling me stuff they think I want to hear.

"My close friends are in Portland, and that's the way it's always going to be. I grew up with a certain clique and I've been with that clique for probably thirteen years now, and I'm always going to be friends with them. My teammates are my friends, but my really close friends are the guys I grew up with, guys who knew me before all this.

"People who just come on to be your friends when you're famous, or rich — they're not real friends."

Erin Cowan is one of those men who help guide Stoudamire's path. And one of those few, real friends whom Stoudamire trusts. At Stoudamire's request, Cowan came from Portland to Toronto to live for the second season, to act as Stoudamire's sounding board and to help handle the myriad business opportunities that arise. An affable, talkative, animated young man, Cowan is like the anti-Stoudamire, and the two make a good pair.

"It's important to have someone like him around for me," says Stoudamire. "He's somebody I trust, someone who knows where I came from, what I'm all about. I'm my own man but it's nice having someone like him around."

Cowan has seen the growth in his best buddy. He's seen him develop from a rather shy rookie into a more savvy second-year star. He's seen Stoudamire come to understand the need for glad-handing, for flashing his smile and letting people get a bit closer. Not too close, mind you. Just close enough.

"I tell him he's got to be a bit more like me," says Cowan. "He doesn't have to open the door wide, just a crack maybe, and I think he sees that."

One Saturday afternoon teaching clinic at the team's practice facility showed Cowan that his friend was beginning to take his advice. It was in the middle of the team's second season, when the losses were mounting and it was starting to look as though the Raptors were just spinning their wheels. Stoudamire was ticked off by the losses, he was tired, and he was getting cranky. On the way to the clinic, the pair got lost; a major road was closed on their familiar route from their downtown home to the practice facility, a fact that only darkened Stoudamire's mood. All he wanted to know was when the clinic would be over. Once they arrived, however — once he started talking to the kids — there was no stopping him.

"They were trying to get him to shut up but he wouldn't," says Cowan. "He kept telling them stories about growing up, he kept telling them basketball things. The guy running the clinic finally got him to stop, took the microphone, but Damon grabbed it right back and was like, 'Hey, hang on. There's some more I gotta say.' It was like a new Damon, and the people running the clinic said they had never seen a better one. After, I told him that's what he's got to be like all the time. He was just having fun."

And learning.

"I remember it, yeah," says Stoudamire. "I don't let a lot of people get close to me and sometimes I'm not too open, but it's getting better. I don't think I'll ever be like some people who just let everyone know everything, but I know what I've got to do at a clinic like that. And in other business dealings."

The off-court dealings aren't all money-makers; some are just profile-raisers or simple good deeds. Stoudamire recognizes the place he has in the hearts of young people, and he knows that, like it or not, athletes are role models, and people want to hear what they have to say. A word from someone like Damon Stoudamire carries a lot of weight.

"Hey, doing stuff for the kids is cool," he says. "If I'm doing a clinic or something with a lot of little kids, that's something I really like. The kids want someone to look up to and someone to spend some time with them, and I like that."

To that end, Stoudamire is heavily involved in the Raptors' excellent community relations initiatives. He's an honorary member of the franchise's Raptors Foundation, which has raised millions of dollars for programs throughout the city and across the country. As part of his rookie of the year win, he set up a $20,000 scholarship fund administered through the Boys and Girls Club of Canada to help financially strapped youngsters continue their education. He's a spokesman for the NBA's Team Up program, a call to action that encourages youth to get involved with, and give back to, their communities through public service. That's one of Stoudamire's favourites, and the public service television announcement that shows him helping out at a children's centre is an indication of how much fun he can have just hanging with kids and helping them grow as people.

He has been involved in the Stay in School program, celebrations of Black History Month, the national committees in Canada and the United States to prevent child abuse and the Reading is Fundamental program.

He took trips to Japan and France to take part in NBA-sponsored instructional clinics where he also helped raise the profile of the sport.

If nothing else, he knows there is a responsibility that comes with his fame, and it's a responsibility he wants to live up to.

Like no other professional sports league, the NBA is one that is driven solely by its stars, and the men who run the show are well aware of that fact. The league office in New York has been described as the best in professional sports because of its marketing abilities and willingness to work unbelievably hard at promoting its best players. The likes of Michael Jordan, Shaquille O'Neal and Charles Barkley are omnipresent, it seems; games aren't the Bulls against the Rockets, they are Michael against Charles; it's Shawn Kemp versus Karl Malone, Grant Hill versus Penny Hardaway. In bygone years, it was Magic Johnson and Larry Bird and Jordan.

These days, even coaches are getting in on the star-making

act. The Indiana Pacers are now Larry Bird and the Indiana Pacers; the Boston Celtics are no longer simply the most storied franchise in league history, they are Rick Pitino and the Boston Celtics. It's a galaxy of stars, and the league office knows it and milks it for all it's worth. The marketing wizards at the NBA office in New York get some help from the media as well, because the television networks know that the names sell the games and the games drive the ratings and the ratings drive the revenue.

So where does Stoudamire fit in? He's definitely in line to be in the next vanguard of marketable commodities, a young player waiting his turn, until the Jordans and Barkleys and Malones are gone. The fact that he plays for a Canadian-based team, especially one that has had little success on the court, isn't helping his overall profile. But once the Raptors start winning consistently, once they become a major contender in the Eastern conference and force themselves into the upper echelon of the league's teams, the little guard will be in a position to move to the centre of a much bigger stage.

Fans in Toronto and across Canada will get the opportunity to witness the transformation that is likely to occur with the Raptors.

"Our time, his time, is coming," says Isiah Thomas. "If the league gets behind you, amazing things can happen, and I think the league will realize he's one of the most exciting young players in the game. If you want excitement, seeing people run up and down the floor, play the game at an incredible pace and make people around you better, he's the man who's going to do that."

The NBA is a billion-dollar worldwide industry that has created wealth for all who come in contact with it. Under strict salary-cap guidelines, teams can spend up to about $25 million on player salaries alone — which works out to an average of more than $2 million per year for every player on the team. That doesn't apply to a player re-signing with his present team who can get whatever he can negotiate. That means teams that are willing to pay exorbitant salaries can tie up their superstars in one city for the duration of their careers. That in turn allows fans to identify with the best players without always worrying about them bolting to another city. Unlike baseball players, who seem to switch teams almost at will, basketball stars tend to be loyal. Isiah Thomas spent all of his eleven seasons with the Detroit Pistons; Larry Bird spent his entire playing career with the Boston Celtics; Magic Johnson was a Laker for life; and Michael Jordan has worn no other NBA uniform than the familiar red, white and black of the Chicago Bulls.

The reliance on superstars to market the game has created some ill will, however, on a couple of levels. There has been an erosion of the middle rank of players — the superstars get all the money, the rest are left scrambling for relative table scraps — and Toronto fans and Stoudamire saw that first-hand. Big centre Oliver Miller bolted after one season with the Raptors, exercising an option in a contract that would have paid him more than $5 million over two seasons in search of a bigger, longer, more lucrative deal. He settled for $247,500 with the Dallas Mavericks, was eventually cut there and ended the 1996–97 season as a man without a contract. That $5 million has gone, and he won't get it back.

If your name becomes synonymous with the next wave of NBA stars, as Stoudamire's has, the sky is absolutely the limit. But if not, watch out. There is a perceived lack of respect for those who haven't made the "A" list. Stoudamire sees it first-hand in nearly every game when the Raptors don't get a vital call from a referee at a key moment. Add in more subtle slights like tougher travel schedules and limiting a team's exposure by keeping it off national television in the United States, and the conspiracy theorists have a field day. It's tough to argue with them. Stoudamire and others think there are forces at work to ensure that the biggest superstars get the biggest breaks in every game they play. Just watch Jordan get away with little things like tugging on an opponent's jersey, or Patrick Ewing sneak in a couple of extra, illegal steps on his post move.

Of course, there are those who think the superstars earn their breaks with their successful track records. If you're the best player in the history of the game, as Jordan is, maybe you should get the benefit of the doubt. If you're a warrior like Ewing, who comes to work every day and gives an honest effort for his pay, maybe little indiscretions should be ignored. If you don't bitch and complain to referees every single time something doesn't go your way, maybe the guys in charge will cut you a little slack. If that's favouritism, so be it; that's just the way the world works.

Things have started to turn a bit for the Raptors and Stoudamire. He used to get hit nearly every time he ventured near the basket and the whistles were silent. Perhaps referees are watching a bit more closely now; perhaps they are just more familiar with his moves. You have to earn your stripes in the NBA, and two seasons of competing gamely have earned the Raptors and Stoudamire a little respect.

"This is just my opinion, but it seems the NBA can keep a team down for as long as they want to, and when they want to build a team back up, they can do it," Stoudamire says.

"I'm a firm believer that we're going to be good when the NBA wants us to be good. We're gonna start winning close games when the NBA wants us to win close games and we're going to start getting close calls when we start winning those close games consistently. I guess it's just a matter of waiting our turn, but it's tough waiting. Sometimes we wonder if we're ever going to get some breaks."

Stoudamire knows the key to fame is staying in one place and taking his team to the top — much the way his general manager did. Financially, it's best to stay put. Because of the overall salary cap, it will be hard for other teams to find the money to pay him the close to $10 million (U.S.) a year he'll command; the Raptors can pay him whatever they want without regard to the cap because he'll be one of Toronto's free agents. But personally, there's nothing that drives him like taking a team from the bottom to the top.

"Hey, I was here when things were terrible, when we were losing all the time and teams didn't fear us. When we get good, I want to be here, and I want people to say I brought the team from the bottom to the top. That's going to be fun, beating the teams that were laughing at us when we were on the bottom. And winning all the time — winning all the time is going to be the most fun."

EPILOGUE

AS THE 1997–98 SEASON DAWNS, the light shines brightly on one of the promising young franchises in the league, and on its star attraction. This will be a season in which expectations previously kept private are laid out for all the world to see. When Damon Stoudamire stood in a parking lot before the 1996–97 season began and announced that he expected to take his team to the playoffs and to make an appearance in the All-Star game, it was a private thought everyone knew in their hearts was little more than a pipe dream. This year, however, he may as well stand on the SkyDome roof and shout the words for all to hear. He, more than anyone else, will let his teammates know and the team's fans know that this is the year the Raptors will make their biggest move.

"We've lost more in the first two seasons than I ever have in my life, and it doesn't feel good," he says. "I know I don't want to put up with that any more, and I don't expect anyone else on the squad will put up with it."

In their first two seasons, the Raptors showed steady, if not dramatic, improvement. Though they started as an expansion team considered little more than a nuisance by the league's best, they've become a franchise to be reckoned with as the future unfolds. Primarily because of Stoudamire's talents, the Raptors have beaten all the best teams in the league at least once — Chicago, Seattle and Orlando in the first year, and Chicago, Utah and Houston in the second. Much to Stoudamire's chagrin, however, they lost to the expansion Vancouver Grizzlies in each of the first two seasons, and three times to the wretched Boston Celtics in year two. It is that kind of inconsistency that rankles the most; the frustration of losses in games the team should win offsets the euphoria of victories over the best teams around. It is the single biggest problem the franchise has had, a maddening inconsistency that leaves all close to it shaking their heads in wonderment.

The Raptors' first season, under the iron fist of coach Brendan Malone, was a learning experience for all involved.

Stoudamire learned the intricacies of the NBA game, he learned how to handle the grind of an eighty-two-game season, he learned how to handle being an NBA star. And he learned a lot about himself — especially how much he hated the relentless losing. He also learned that all the skills he knew he had were good enough to carry him to the league's upper echelon. He wasn't too short, he wasn't too weak. Those fans who booed his selection on draft night in June 1995 were wrong, and Isiah Thomas was right.

"I don't think Damon gets enough credit for helping create awareness of our team and our sport," says Isiah Thomas. "He *is* the Raptors. He is the player they all remember. He brought a level of excitement to the game every night that not many people expected or thought possible."

One of the biggest fears of a new franchise in any professional sport is the second season. First years are honeymoons: everyone likes everything — from the players to the uniforms to the stadiums to the T-shirts. There are no expectations placed on teams and, because they are often bad, that's something to be thankful for. In year two, however, the dynamic changes.

If there is any sign of promise in a first season, the expectations of fans and players rise exponentially. "See?" they say: "We're a good team, we can make a huge step because we're not an expansion team any more. We'll be right there, watch us."

The folly of that thought often becomes apparent quickly. The sports history books are littered with stories about teams that have taken gigantic steps backwards in their second season — partly because the opponents who cruised against a first-year team step it up the next time around, partly because the hunger that drives a first-year team searching for respectability diminishes. To the credit of the Raptors, and their on-court leader, that didn't happen. The Raptors went from 21 wins their first year to 30 their second, a jump that might have been just 9 of 82 games in the standings but that was huge for the team's psyche. As a comparison, the Vancouver Grizzlies won 15 games in their first year but just 14 in the second season. It's that kind of dangerous slide — which raises questions about the players and the organization that sometimes lead to panic firings and trades — that the Raptors have avoided.

"It'll be a gradual process, but once we get to the top, we're going to stay there," says Stoudamire. "I don't think we'll fall to rock bottom. We might slide to the middle of the pack and not be the champions every year, but we'll be in the hunt. We won't go back to rock bottom. We've already been there."

Stoudamire's second season was more or less an extension of his first. He averaged more than 20 points a game and finished with more than 9 assists a night. He was part of some disheartening losses, but he battled every time he was on the floor, and led the team to some spectacular wins as well. Stoudamire left

Toronto after the season feeling good about himself, good about his teammates and good about the future.

Stoudamire also feels buoyed by the stability that has come to the front office. In order to attract players, attract a paying audience, and attract businesses willing to invest their money, stability at the top and a saleable product is hugely important. Stability has not been one of the buzzwords floating around the franchise.

When Isiah Thomas reached an agreement in principle to obtain majority control of the team, it ensured that he would remain in place as the director of the basketball operation and cleared up an ownership situation that had been muddled from the start of the team's second season.

"One of the reasons I don't think we'll ever hit rock bottom like the first two years is that Isiah's here," says Stoudamire. "If he wasn't here, we would hit rock bottom again because there aren't enough basketball heads in the organization to know what's going on. If we had any other general manager, there's no question this franchise would fall back to right where it was in the first two years, trying to get good."

The Raptors will also have to try to overcome their home arena, which doesn't provide many comforts.

Two years in the SkyDome is two too many for most of the players, and there is at least one more to come. The concrete egg at the bottom of the city's downtown core might be a nice baseball park and a passable concert hall, but it just can't provide the intimacy needed for basketball. In the NBA, more than in any other sport, a home-court advantage is palpable; visiting teams are affected by the crowd, and even physical details like the tightness of the rims on the baskets lend a break to the home team. Because the Raptors can't even practise regularly at their own facility, because they have to continually schlep their stuff from the SkyDome locker room to their practice facility miles away, the Raptors feel like homeless pros. Stoudamire hates packing up his locker at the SkyDome, dragging all his stuff to Glendon College and doing it all over again up to twice a week. Professional athletes are creatures of habit, and it's hard to develop habits when you're sharing your home with a baseball team, a football team and the likes of "The Three Tenors."

The Raptors had originally planned to spend just two seasons in the Dome, but that plan changed as often as the ownership structure. The dream of an intimate, basketball-only arena helped sell the league's expansion committee even before the franchise was awarded; later, that plan changed, and the team was going to move to a former postal building at the foot of Bay Street. That idea lasted for a couple of years, until Thomas was able to do what neither John Bitove nor Allan Slaight had been able to pull off: he found some common ground for discussion with the NHL's Maple Leafs. Every sane-thinking sports fan in Toronto knew that one new arena for two teams would be a logical business proposition.

All the business dealings, all the boardroom shenanigans, all the arena follies are secondary, however, to what Stoudamire is all about — playing ball. It is how he has made his mark throughout his life, it's how he will make his mark in the future. His accomplishments as a player will be his legacy, not whether an arena is built or how the team's ownership is constructed. If he continues to be the high-scoring point guard who takes charge whenever he's on the floor, if he makes himself into an even more important offensive force by developing a slashing, get-to-the basket game where he can kick the ball back out to consistently sharp-shooting teammates, the Raptors will continue to improve. Nothing he has shown in his first two years suggests he won't.

For the franchise, 1997–98 will be a watershed year. The team's mission statement sets out a lofty, yet simple goal: "The Toronto Raptors are committed to delivering the most exciting, value-focused entertainment experience in Canada, while producing a winning team capable of NBA championships, and contributing to the promotion and development of basketball, at all levels, in Canada and around the world for the benefit of our fans, shareholders and employees." That is a long, difficult journey that, as they say, must begin with small steps.

Stoudamire will come back from his summer vacation revitalized, having devoted himself to off-season workouts and making improvements to his game. Sort of like a big brother checking up on his siblings, Stoudamire keeps close tabs on his teammates in the off-season, urging them, too, to work on the parts of their game that need the most development. Thomas set up a little mini-camp for the team over a long weekend in Chicago in late May that provided a perfect opportunity for Stoudamire to encourage them to stay focused on their goals. "It's up to them to work on their games but when we get together, we can remind them," Stoudamire said.

At every step in his growth, from a little boy lying on his grandmother's living-room floor looking at the pictures in the paper to standing in the spotlight as a bona fide NBA star, Damon Stoudamire has met the challenges and reached his goals.

He once watched NBA stars glide across his television screen and dreamed of the day he would be in the league, be a player. He made himself into that player, got himself to the league, and he stands now on the verge of greatness.

Isiah Thomas and the Toronto Raptors gambled when they chose Stoudamire as the man around whom their franchise would be built. That gamble looks like a sure bet right now, a testament to the heart and desire of the man with the Mighty Mouse tattoo.

Damon Stoudamire always knew there was a place for him in the NBA. Now, the NBA and its fans know it as well.

Damon Stoudamire's

GAME-BY-GAME STATS

1995–96 season

GAME		POINTS	ASSISTS	SCORE
1	New Jersey	10 points	10 assists	94-79 win.
2	at Indiana	26 points	11 assists	97-89 loss.
3	at Chicago	22 points	10 assists	117-108 loss.
4	Sacramento	8 points	2 assists	109-90 loss.
5	Phoenix	22 points	7 assists	112-108 loss.
6	at Charlotte	12 points	1 assist	123-117 loss (OT).
7	Utah	7 points	9 assists	103-100 loss.
8	Houston	20 points	9 assists	96-93 loss.
9	Minnesota	20 points	13 assists	114-96 win.
10	at Washington	23 points	10 assists	103-102 loss.
11	Seattle	20 points	11 assists	102-97 win.
12	at Milwaukee	7 points	9 assists	96-86 loss.
13	at Atlanta	18 points	9 assists	114-102 loss.
14	Golden State	18 points	10 assists	101-98 loss.
15	at Cleveland	18 points	4 assists	93-89 loss.
16	Philadelphia	15 points	10 assists	105-102 win.
17	Miami	13 points	15 assists	112-94 loss.
18	at Seattle	10 points	5 assists	119-89 loss.
19	at Portland	15 points	10 assists	96-88 loss.
20	at LA Lakers	20 points	10 assists	120-103 loss.

GAME		POINTS	ASSISTS	SCORE
21	at Vancouver	24 points	8 assists	93-81 win.
22	Boston	18 points	9 assists	116-96 loss.
23	Indiana	13 points	13 assists	102-100 loss.
24	at Boston	15 points	7 assists	122-103 loss.
25	Orlando	21 points	10 assists	110-93 win.
26	Detroit	19 points	8 assists	94-82 loss.
27	at Chicago	20 points	13 assists	113-104 loss.
28	at New York	25 points	8 assists	103-91 loss.
29	Milwaukee	21 points	11 assists	93-87 win.
30	at Detroit	27 points	7 assists	113-91 loss.
31	at Orlando	23 points	13 assists	121-110 loss.
32	at Atlanta	19 points	10 assists	104-101 loss (OT).
33	Charlotte	20 points	8 assists	92-91 loss.
34	Atlanta	18 points	9 assists	87-79 loss.
35	Washington	29 points	11 assists	106-100 win.
36	at New Jersey	18 points	11 assists	108-83 loss.
37	Indiana	29 points	10 assists	110-102 loss.
38	Chicago	26 points	12 assists	92-89 loss.
39	Boston	23 points	9 assists	97-95 win.
40	New Jersey	11 points	11 assists	86-79 win.
41	Vancouver	22 points	12 assists	106-101 loss (OT).
42	at Denver	23 points	5 assists	93-82 loss.

GAME		POINTS	ASSISTS	SCORE
43	at Sacramento	4 points	6 assists	102-75 loss.
44	at Golden State	25 points	11 assists	114-111 loss.
45	at LA Clippers	25 points	6 assists	119-113 win (OT).
46	Portland	16 points	7 assists	90-87 loss.
47	Milwaukee	12 points	6 assists	93-88 loss.
48	at Miami	29 points	7 assists	98-87 win.
49	Cleveland	8 points	7 assists	95-76 loss.
50	at Detroit	13 points	9 assists	108-95 loss.
51	at Utah	23 points	6 assists	102-86 loss.
52	at Phoenix	29 points	10 assists	110-105 loss.
53	at Dallas	23 points	10 assists	105-98 loss.
54	at Houston	17 points	19 assists	105-100 loss.
55	at San Antonio	10 points	5 assists	120-95 loss.
56	at Cleveland	24 points	2 assists	100-89 win.
57	Detroit	15 points	6 assists	105-84 loss.
58	New York	14 points	15 assists	89-82 loss.
59	at Miami	11 points	5 assists	109-79 loss.
60	Dallas	25 points	9 assists	128-112 win.
61	at Philadelphia	did not play (stomach virus)		118-110 loss.
62	at Charlotte	20 points	11 assists	113-101 loss.
63	at Indiana	23 points	12 assists	105-96 loss.
64	Denver	14 points	16 assists	122-114 loss.

GAME		POINTS	ASSISTS	SCORE
65	Charlotte	24 points	10 assists	107-89 win.
66	San Antonio	23 points	13 assists	120-108 loss.
67	Chicago	30 points	11 assists	109-108 win.
68	Atlanta	30 points	12 assists	114-111 loss.
69	at Philadelphia	did not play (tendinitis)		103-94 loss.
70	Orlando	15 points	5 assists	120-86 loss.
71	LA Lakers	19 points	15 assists	111-106 loss.
72	LA Clippers	29 points	12 assists	104-103 win (OT).
73	Cleveland	did not play (tendinitis)		98-77 loss.
74	New York	did not play (tendinitis)		139-106 loss.
75	at Minnesota	did not play (tendinitis)		115-101 loss.
76	at Milwaukee	did not play (tendinitis)		102-96 win.
77	at Boston	did not play (tendinitis)		136-108 loss.
78	at Washington	did not play (tendinitis)		110-97 loss.
79	at New York	did not play (tendinitis)		125-79 loss.
80	at New Jersey	did not play (tendinitis)		107-95 loss.
81	Washington	did not play (tendinitis)		107-103 win.
82	Philadelphia	did not play (tendinitis)		109-105 loss (OT).

SEASON TOTALS

Averages per game	19.0 points	9.3 assists	21-61 won-lost record

HIGHLIGHTS

of the 1995–96 season

NAMED NBA ROOKIE OF THE YEAR, earning 76 of a possible 113 votes in balloting by media members in the United States and Canada.

MOST VALUABLE PLAYER in rookie all-star game with 19 points, 11 assists and four steals, the only unanimous selection to NBA's all-rookie team in voting by league coaches.

TIED OR LED THE TEAM IN SCORING 35 times, assists 64 times and minutes played 47 times; had 37 double-doubles (double figures in two offensive categories) and one triple-double (20 points, 12 rebounds, 11 assists vs. Seattle, Nov. 21).

AVERAGED 40.9 MINUTES, seventh highest total by a rookie in NBA history behind Hall of Famers Wilt Chamberlain, Elvin Hayes, Kareem Abdul-Jabbar, Oscar Robertson, Walt Bellamy and Jerry Lucas.

TWO-TIME WINNER of NBA rookie of the month award, in November and January.

SET RECORD for three-point field goals made by a rookie, at 133.

Damon Stoudamire's
GAME-BY-GAME STATS
1996–97 season

GAME		POINTS	ASSISTS	SCORE
1	New York	28 points	10 assists	107-99 loss.
2	at Charlotte	19 points	5 assists	109-98 loss.
3	Dallas	28 points	8 assists	100-96 win.
4	LA Lakers	21 points	10 assists	93-92 win.
5	Denver	13 points	6 assists	104-93 win.
6	Philadelphia	21 points	12 assists	110-96 win.
7	at New York	26 points	13 assists	99-96 loss.
8	at Orlando	17 points	5 assists	92-87 loss.
9	Seattle	did not play (callous on right foot)		
10	Cleveland	24 points	6 assists	89-81 loss.
11	Atlanta	22 points	8 assists	91-88 loss.
12	Sacramento	27 points	6 assists	98-87 loss.
13	Charlotte	10 points	6 assists	92-88 win.
14	at Minnesota	20 points	4 assists	79-70 loss.
15	Houston	27 points	11 assists	100-89 win.
16	at Cleveland	11 points	11 assists	93-74 loss.
17	Washington	12 points	9 assists	82-80 win.
18	at Atlanta	14 points	3 assists	101-75 loss.
19	Chicago	31 points	13 assists	97-89 win.

GAME		POINTS	ASSISTS	SCORE
20	Golden State	19 points	10 assists	101-91 loss.
21	at Boston	31 points	12 assists	115-113 loss (3 OT).
22	at Miami	11 points	4 assists	89-88 loss.
23	Detroit	28 points	8 assists	98-92 loss.
24	at New Jersey	17 points	2 assists	97-88 win.
25	Milwaukee	19 points	12 assists	96-93 win.
26	at Cleveland	14 points	7 assists	91-82 loss.
27	at Indiana	8 points	3 assists	111-92 loss.
28	New Jersey	18 points	6 assists	98-96 win.
29	at Washington	16 points	8 assists	100-82 loss.
30	at Orlando	32 points	12 assists	96-94 loss (OT).
31	at Detroit	4 points	5 assists	118-74 loss.
32	LA Clippers	25 points	9 assists	87-80 loss.
33	Utah	27 points	7 assists	110-96 win.
34	at New Jersey	28 points	9 assists	123-106 win.
35	Orlando	19 points	14 assists	88-85 loss.
36	at Seattle	6 points	7 assists	122-78 loss.
37	at Portland	24 points	3 assists	94-92 win.
38	at Vancouver	34 points	6 assists	100-92 loss.
39	Minnesota	12 points	17 assists	118-106 win.
40	Miami	22 points	11 assists	99-87 loss.
41	at Chicago	28 points	11 assists	110-98 loss.

GAME		POINTS	ASSISTS	SCORE
42	Portland	11 points	13 assists	120-84 win.
43	at Philadelphia	25 points	5 assists	101-99 loss.
44	Phoenix	7 points	13 assists	110-86 win.
45	Boston	26 points	10 assists	114-102 loss.
46	Cleveland	19 points	10 assists	89-84 win.
47	at Milwaukee	13 points	12 assists	1011-96 loss.
48	at Atlanta	15 points	3 assists	106-84 loss.
49	Milwaukee	12 points	14 assists	106-102 loss.
50	Detroit	14 points	15 assists	92-89 loss.
51	at Indiana	23 points	11 assists	105-103 loss.
52	at San Antonio	21 points	9 assists	125-92 win.
53	at Houston	17 points	7 assists	107-97 loss.
54	at Dallas	15 points	9 assists	99-92 win.
55	at Denver	35 points	5 assists	124-122 win (OT).
56	at Utah	14 points	8 assists	118-114 loss.
57	at LA Clippers	22 points	5 assists	94-92 loss.
58	Boston	11 points	17 assists	107-103 loss.
59	New York	22 points	8 assists	100-94 loss.
60	San Antonio	25 points	7 assists	106-103 loss.
61	Vancouver	14 points	10 assists	81-77 win.
62	at Phoenix	22 points	9 assists	105-101 win.
63	at Sacramento	31 points	6 assists	103-96 win.

GAME		POINTS	ASSISTS	SCORE
64	at Golden State	18 points	14 assists	106-102 loss.
65	at LA Lakers	25 points	8 assists	98-90 loss (OT).
66	Philadelphia	30 points	12 assists	117-105 win.
67	at Detroit	9 points	4 assists	99-97 win.
68	Charlotte	29 points	6 assists	102-97 loss.
69	Atlanta	11 points	9 assists	90-79 loss.
70	Indiana	15 points	6 assists	98-84 loss.
71	Chicago	18 points	12 assists	96-83 loss.
72	at Washington	14 points	3 assists	113-86 loss.
73	Miami	35 points	11 assists	102-97 win.
74	at Philadelphia	23 points	15 assists	112-90 win.
75	at Miami	25 points	7 assists	98-84 loss.
76	Washington	29 points	13 assists	100-94 win.
77	Orlando	6 points	5 assists	105-69 loss.
78	Indiana	22 points	11 assists	100-89 loss.
79	at Chicago	29 points	12 assists	117-100 loss.
80	at Milwaukee	11 points	11 assists	92-85 loss.
81	at Charlotte	28 points	9 assists	108-100 win.
82	at Boston	32 points	6 assists	125-94 win.

SEASON TOTALS

Averages per game		20.2 points	8.8 assists	30-52 won-lost record

HIGHLIGHTS

of the 1996–97 season

ONE OF ONLY FOUR GUARDS to rank among league leaders in five statistical categories: scoring (20.2 points per game, 20th), assists (8.8 per game, 6th), free throw percentage (82.3, 28th), steals (1.52, 29th) and minutes per game (40.9, 4th). Others were Michael Jordan, Lattrell Sprewell, Kevin Johnson.

LED TORONTO in scoring, assists, free throw percentage and minutes played.

LED TORONTO in scoring on 39 occasions and in assists 72 times.

TWICE HAD CAREER-HIGH 35-point games, March 30 vs. Miami and Nov. 8 vs. L.A. Lakers.

HAD 33 DOUBLE-DOUBLES (double figures in two offensive statistical categories) and two triple-doubles (against L.A. Lakers — 21 points, 10 assists, 10 rebounds on Nov. 8; and against Philadelphia — 30 points, 10 assists, 12 rebounds on March 18).

FINISHED NINTH in the NBA with 176 three-point field goal attempts.